Using Outdoor Learning to Improve Behaviour for All

Using Outdoor Learning to Improve Behaviour for All focuses on teachers, parents and carers working together and creating environments in the classroom, home and particularly outdoors, where all children can experience positive feedback and develop good learning behaviours.

It tells the story of the Wellie Wednesday project and the journeys children took with their families and schools to achieve success. Based on attachment theory and research in psychology and neuroscience, this practical book will support practitioners, parents, carers and children, who find themselves in negative cycles and situations, to take steps forward to a positive future.

Focusing on real situations and the needs of individual children and their families, this accessible guide is divided into four sections:

- Making a difference: for individual children, their parents, carers and schools.
- Can I be included? Case studies, including impact on family and school, strategies used, changes noticed and key questions raised.
- Addressing concerns: understanding behaviour as communication.
- How change happened: enriching learning to improve behaviour.

Offering a wide collection of case studies and practical strategies, *Using Outdoor Learning to Improve Behaviour for All* will be an essential resource for all teachers, parents and carers wanting to support and guide children towards accessing education successfully.

Sarah Rockliff worked as an advisory support teacher specialising in preventing exclusion. She successfully translated theoretical knowledge into sound practice, changing thinking and behaviour. She worked closely with staff and families to find solutions and meet children's needs.

Pauline Chinnery worked as a headteacher in Norfolk, UK. Her commitment and determination to support children's social and emotional needs resulted in a nurturing ethos across the school and a successful Nurture Group.

Using Outdoor Learning to Improve Behaviour for All

Taking the Wellie Wednesday
journey together

Sarah Rockliff and Pauline Chinnery

Routledge
Taylor & Francis Group

LONDON AND NEW YORK

First published 2016
by Routledge
2 Park Square, Milton Park, Abingdon, Oxon OX14 4RN

and by Routledge
711 Third Avenue, New York, NY 10017

Routledge is an imprint of the Taylor & Francis Group, an informa business

British Library Cataloguing in Publication Data
A catalogue record for this book is available from the British Library

Library of Congress Cataloging in Publication Data
Rockliff, Sarah.
Using outdoor learning to improve behaviour for all : taking the Wellie Wednesday journey together / Sarah Rockliff and Pauline Chinnery.
pages cm
ISBN 978-1-138-94287-5 -- ISBN 978-1-138-94288-2 -- ISBN 978-1-315-67287-8
1. Outdoor education--Great Britain. 2. Behavior modification--Great Britain. 3. Marginality, Social--Great Britain. I. Chinnery, Pauline. II. Title.
LC1038.8.G7R63 2016
371.3'84--dc23
2015022262

ISBN: 978-1-138-94287-5 (hbk)
ISBN: 978-1-138-94288-2 (pbk)
ISBN: 978-1-315-67287-8 (ebk)

Typeset in Sabon
by Saxon Graphics Ltd, Derby
Printed in Great Britain by Ashford Colour Press Ltd

Contents

Acknowledgements

Our thanks to all the children who have enriched and informed our working lives. We never failed to be moved, delighted and inspired by the changes we witnessed.

Initial referrals from schools for children to join the Wellie Wednesday project often painted daunting pictures of real and worrying concerns. Together, difficulties were faced, challenges were tackled and perceptions altered. Hard work, determination, insight and experience, contributed willingly by a dedicated team of staff and volunteers, provided role models for the participants. They were able to experience cooperative working, problem-solving and the benefits of group connectedness. Adults and children alike experienced moments of awe and wonder in the outdoor setting, and shared joy, warmth, fun and laughter. We were heartened by the resilience, charm, trust and affection that the children invested in changing their thinking and behaviour. The parents and carers who joined the groups showed open mindedness and a willingness to find different ways of interacting with their children in order to move forward from difficult times. Our heartfelt thanks to all of you.

We are grateful to so many people for their encouragement, support for and enthusiasm for the project.

Teamwork was at the core of our success; we feel privileged that individuals were willing to put in so much physical, emotional and good-humoured commitment to be part of the team. To these excellent colleagues and superb volunteers: thank you; you made a safe, welcoming and secure base for our families. They experienced so much that was new, but with your help, felt safe to experiment with change in order to find their preferred futures.

To our line managers, Liz Jones and Tom Burt, who always had faith in the idea of us trying something completely different, we thank you for believing and trusting in us.

Thank you to the specialist support assistants, who even before the project was conceived, took on new ways of group working and were crucial to the development of what became the Wellie Wednesday project. Their support and interest in using fresh ideas to make a difference to vulnerable children contributed to the background of the project. The small group work and residential camp that took place at Ranworth First School provided another formative part of the development of Wellie Wednesday. Our thanks to the enthusiastic staff who were involved. The success of these camps contributed to our decision to use the outdoor environment to offer an alternative context for adults and children learning together.

A special mention of thanks to specialist teaching assistant, Julie Edwards, whose commitment and expertise were an invaluable support to every session.

To John Rockliff, who was volunteered by us for the project: thank you! He came willingly and enthusiastically and not only gave us moral support but made important additions to the overall experience of the project, including driving the minibus. John's skills with cooking on a fire inspired children and adults alike; his imaginative menus, food shopping and preparation ensured that mealtimes were always central to the day's enjoyment. An enormous task, but there was always enough food for everyone, served on time, and each week there were enthusiastic compliments to the chef.

We were pleased to expand our team at times to include additional professionals, who showed interest and excitement about the project. We thank you all, especially Jessica Pitt, for contributing an additional depth of knowledge by using music to enrich the Wellie Wednesday experience and embed the messages in a motivating way.

We are grateful to Shirley, who delighted the children and adults by producing a booklet of 'John's Marvellous Menus' for each of them, enlivened with their own enthusiastic comments.

Thank you to the managers of the outdoor centre, Kevin Hart and John McKean, who welcomed the families and embraced the ethos of the project. They contributed their interest, time and knowledge to enhance the children's learning and enjoyment of the natural world. Kevin introduced us to Meg the sheepdog, who will always be fondly remembered; a most unusual role model who demonstrated following instructions as she and Kevin worked together with the sheep. Children enjoyed and benefited from John's informal and encouraging conversations, as well as the much-enjoyed informative activities, including marvelling at the age of a tree by carefully counting its rings, dipping into the pond to discover its wildlife and feeding the red squirrels and the sheep.

Without headteachers, who became excited about finding a positive way forward for their troubled young people, there would have been no Wellie Wednesday. We met inspirational and dedicated teachers and assistants, we found schools willing to go to great lengths with us to find ways for vulnerable children to succeed. Every child needed a key person to welcome them back each Thursday, to listen to their recounting of the previous day's activities, and above all to take on the strategies, so that learning was successfully transferred into school. These people were key to the success of the individual children; they too were willing to take on the Wellie Wednesday ethos even though they had not been a part of the sessions. Their collaboration was crucial and ensured that the children continued to make progress. We cannot thank by name all of the many people involved, but you know who you are and we remember you with affection and gratitude.

This book has been written in response to requests for us to record our ways of working with children and their families. From Norfolk, we thank Dr Lesley Ashby, Dr Teresa Belton and Rosemary Games, for their positive and affirming feedback; from Ottawa, Dr Jane Miller, for offering a knowledgeable and objective view. We gained great confidence from their encouraging comments, which gave us further incentive to continue.

Finally, our thanks to John Rockliff and Doug Chinnery for their ongoing, unfailing, support and encouragement during the writing of this book. It has been an exciting new development of our work and we are grateful to all those who have encouraged us along the way.

Introduction

You are here not just to find out who you are, but who you want to be.

(Theraplay UK)

'Wellie Wednesday' was developed as a progressive personal and social education programme that focused on the needs of individual children and their families. It provided an outdoor environmental experience where children enjoyed and appreciated the countryside, developed thinking skills, worked within a positive group and experienced social, physical and cognitive challenges. Through introducing children to a wider world and enjoying moments of awe and wonder, the project broadened their horizons and raised aspirations.

The team was made up of a group of professionals: teachers, headteachers, teaching assistants and others with a wealth experience, including the volunteer cook and managers of the outdoor centre where the project was held. The team had come together with a common passionate interest and total commitment to introducing positive change for children and their families who were struggling within challenging situations relating to the children's school experiences.

The schools were selected because they were keen to try an alternative approach. They showed enthusiastic commitment and were willing to take forward the ideas and strategies introduced. Some staff from the schools attended the sessions to experience first hand the ethos and strategies used by the team.

The parents and carers were chosen to take part because they were keen to become involved and to try an alternative approach to support their children's needs, to facilitate change and take steps towards a positive future. They were keen to attend with their children to learn new approaches to conflict situations. They were receptive to working with others, and to giving and receiving support.

The children selected for the project were identified as being at risk of exclusion. Some children had experienced fixed-term exclusions, some were excluded and some were only attending school on a part-time basis. All children were identified as having significant social, emotional and behavioural needs, often linked to poor attachment. In some cases, these were children in care (looked-after children) and adopted children. A variety of other strategies had already been tried at home and at school but had failed to support their high level of need. These children required an alternative learning environment to support schools in meeting their needs.

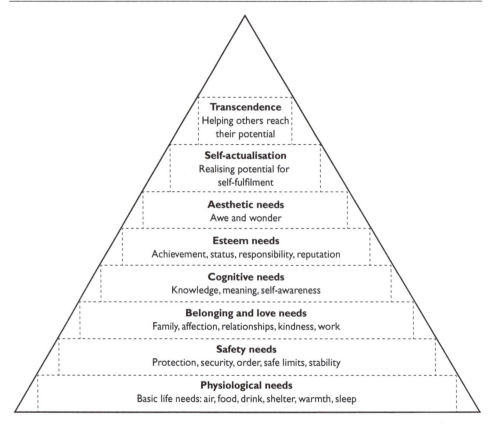

Figure 0.1 Hierarchy of needs inspired by Maslow.

It was evident that the selected children were failing to access the curriculum successfully because of their unmet needs, either emotionally, developmentally or cognitively. As Maslow's hierarchy of needs (Maslow 1954, updated 1970) indicates, only when the foundations upon which mainstream learning depends are in place, can the child fully access education successfully.

The project was developed for children between the ages of six and eight years and their parents or carers. Taking part in a developmentally appropriate intervention enabled them to acquire the emotional readiness required to access education successfully. The success of the intervention relied on using evidence-based methodology translated by the team into child-friendly opportunities.

It incorporated the following foundations, which were developed from The National Primary Behaviour and Attendance Strategy 2005 Pilot, small group work for vulnerable children and their parents:

- Maslow's Hierarchy of Needs.
- Nurture Group theory: A child who has not experienced satisfactory emotional, social and cognitive development in the earliest years will not be able to engage with normal age appropriate school provision (Bennathan and Boxall 1998).

- Attachment and attunement theory: 'safe place', use of transitional objects, playfulness, acceptance, curiosity and empathy (PACE) (Hughes 2006), recognition of the importance of parental involvement.
- Cognitive development through enriched and mediated learning; changing the way children think (Feuerstein et al. 1980).
- Solution-focused approaches to engender optimism by finding solutions rather than focusing on the problem (de Shazer 1998).
- Narrative therapy approach to problem-solving: externalising the problems allowing children to acknowledge self-worth (see Chapter 10) (Morgan 1999).
- Developing a vocabulary of feelings: PATHS (Promoting alternative thinking strategies) (Greenberg and Kusche 1995) – enables children to move beyond communicating distress through challenging behaviour.

Further details can be found in Chapter 18.

The project provided a progressive learning experience, building skills and confidence through mastery of increasingly complex tasks. Parents, carers and children experienced success and learnt to encourage and cooperate. Challenges were devised to develop sensory and motor systems to improve coordination and self-regulation.
    The project was based on the belief that children need to experience:

- A sense of belonging: A positive social setting in order to thrive. Being part of an encouraging group helps to build cooperation, affection, trust and loyalty, leading to a sense of self-worth.
- Acceptance: A separation needs to be made between the child and their difficult behaviour. 'We always like and care about you, we don't always like your behaviour.' Children need to know they are liked, even when their behaviour is challenging.
- Reciprocity: Our feelings have an impact on other people. Expressing and experiencing positive feelings towards each other can result in shared pleasure.
- Emotional warmth: Children need to know they are liked and that their opinions and feelings are valued.
- Security: A base from which to safely grow in confidence and gain independence.

The aims of the project were as follows:

- To build a supportive team around each child and primary carer.
- To provide comfort and reassurance to children who had been troubled at school.
- To offer practical, supportive and positive advice and ideas to parents and carers.
- To offer professional and alternative ideas to teachers and teaching assistants in school.
- To ensure everyone felt included and valued; to create an ethos that promoted feelings of acceptance and respect.
- To awaken children's curiosity; to introduce the group to the wider world, where it was hoped that they would develop a sense of awe and wonder; to transcend into a new world of possibilities.
- To establish a more positive approach to school for children and their primary carers.

- To offer experiential learning in a nurturing and enriching outdoor environment.
- To focus on the present and the future, whilst acknowledging the impact of early trauma.
- To enable times of quiet to be experienced positively and to explore 'beautiful thoughts'.
- To ensure children felt safe to take on new experiences and challenges.
- To create and maintain a sense of group cohesion and to promote positive interactions.
- To ensure, through careful planning, that a range of stimulating activities were introduced to the group to meet their needs and to establish group identity, cooperation, responsibility and raise self-esteem.
- To build up a positive picture, a sense of self, for each person, through the language of compliments.
- To set targets; to notice and celebrate what children were getting right.

Children need to be able to recognise what contributes to their own success. The following list offers some ideas from a child's perspective:

I will know I am successful when I can...
- join in
- express emotion appropriately
- cope with change
- deal with disappointment
- accept direction
- follow instruction
- enjoy excitement appropriately
- think before I do, say before I do
- wait for a turn
- share equipment
- manage frustration when things go wrong
- accept not knowing
- praise and encourage others
- be trusted with equipment
- make appropriate choices
- work and play independently
- be kind to myself and others
- feel proud of myself.

About this book

This book describes the developmental journey for a selection of children as they took part in the Wellie Wednesday project. The experience enabled them to take steps along a positive pathway with support from the team, their parent or carer and the school. We hope other children and adults will be able to make similar journeys using our experiences as a starting point.

Making a difference: for individual children, their parents, carers and schools

Chapter 1 describes the aims of the project and how it evolved in practice, building a picture of the Wellie Wednesday project. Chapter 2 outlines the valued contribution of parents, carers and other significant adults, without whose commitment the project would not have been successful.

Can I be included? Case studies, including impact on family and school, strategies used, changes noticed and key questions raised

Chapters 3–8 are case studies of children, with a particular focus on their specific needs and how the children were supported. Their strengths and difficulties were the starting point based on information from schools and home. Specific strategies are described, along with details of progress made.

Addressing concerns: understanding behaviour as communication

Chapters 9–14 outline particular areas of difficulty experienced by a number of children, which had previously resulted in negative outcomes at school and at home. Chapter 15 describes a range of responses to food and the significance on children's well-being and anxiety levels. It acknowledges how strong emotional responses can impact on adults and children.

How change happened: enriching learning to improve behaviour

Chapter 16 gives an overview of the strategies used to enable inclusion in school and provides a quick reference for practitioners, parents and carers who find themselves in challenging situations with children who are troubled in school or at home.

Chapter 17 describes ways in which parents and carers were supported, gained confidence in themselves and developed an increased understanding of their children's behaviour as a means of communication.

Chapter 18: explains the theoretical background.

The final chapter, the Conclusion, demonstrates how the learning from Wellie Wednesday continued to have an impact. This chapter emphasises that the rural environment provided the vehicle for vital learning to take place in order to facilitate change: a new positive view of self, a new positive approach to challenge, a new way of managing anxiety, a new way of thinking and being.

Epilogue: the way we would like it to be for all children.

You believed in me so I could start to believe in myself.

(YMCA resident)

References

Bennathan, M. and Boxall, M. (1998). *The Boxall profile: A guide to effective intervention in the education of pupils with emotional and behavioural difficulties; Handbook for teachers.* Nurture Group Consortium; Association of Workers for Children with Emotional and Behavioural Difficulties. Maidstone: AWCEBD.

De Shazer, S. (1998). *Key to solution in brief therapy.* New York: Norton.

Feuerstein, R., Feuerstein, R., Falik, L.H. and Rand, Y. (1980). *Instrumental enrichment.* Baltimore: University Park Press.

Greenberg, M. and Kusche, C. (1995). *Promoting alternative thinking strategies (PATHS).* South Deerfield: Channing Bete Company.

Hughes, D. (2006). *Building the bonds of attachment.* New York: J. Aronson Inc. Publishers.

Maslow, A.H. (1954). *Motivation and personality.* New York: Harper. Second Ed, New York: Harper (1970); Third Ed, New York: Harper (1987).

Morgan, A. (Ed) (1999). *Once upon a time: Narrative therapy with children and their families.* Adelaide: Dulwich Centre Publications.

Chapter 1

Building a picture of Wellie Wednesday

He drew a circle that shut me out – heretic, rebel, a thing to flout. But love and I had the will to win: we drew a circle that took him in!

(Edwin Markham)

How it seems to me...
When I am shouted at, I want to shout back.
When I am told to hurry, I want to go slower.
When I am stopped, I want to bite or kick.
When I see a door, I want to run.
When I see a table, I want to go under it.
When I see a chair, I want to knock it over.
When I see a window, I want to climb out.
When I am given a task, I want to mess it up.
When I am asked to write, I throw things.

When someone shows kindness, compassion and understanding, then I am curious.
I try, and begin to get things right.
When I see trees, I want to explore.
When I hear birds, I enjoy listening.
When I belong, I can enjoy having fun.
When I feel safe, I can make mistakes.
When I feel valued, I can join in.
When I am given time, I can understand.
When I am understood, I can think more clearly.
When people believe in me, I feel I can do it.
When others are kind to me, I want to be kind too.

(P. Chinnery and S. Rockliff)

Setting up the project

When the Wellie Wednesday project was set up, the aim was to build a supportive team around each child and their primary carer; to provide comfort and reassurance to children who had become troubled at school; to offer practical, supportive and positive advice and ideas to the parent or carer; to offer professional and alternative ideas to the teachers and teaching assistants in school. The aim was to ensure that everyone felt included and valued. The diagram, Concentric circles of experience (Figure 1.1), uses concentric circles to represent the interconnection between the individual's need for a secure base and sense of belonging, in order to successfully engage with the wider world.

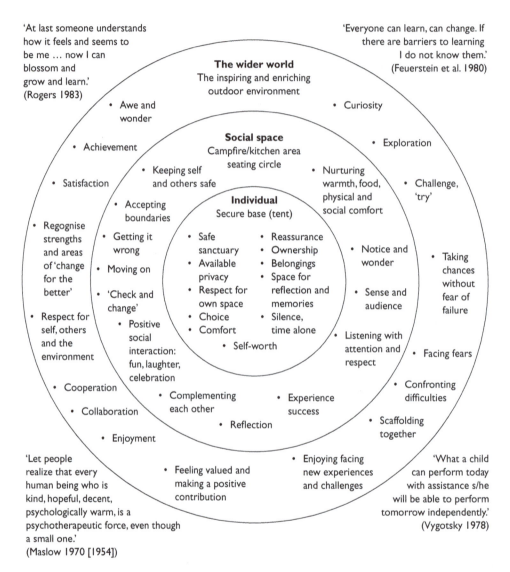

Figure 1.1 Concentric circles of experience.

Source: © Authors.

Foundations of the project

For some children, the school environment can seem threatening and trigger negative responses, preventing them from learning. Through the project the children's curiosity about learning was awakened, resulting in a more positive approach to school.

At Wellie Wednesday, an environment for learning was created for families that was different from their previous experience; it offered experiential learning in a nurturing and enriching outdoor environment. The structuring of the project was based upon previous work. It had been noticed that a school camping trip for a class of seven- to eight-year-old children had brought about considerable change in relationships and self-esteem. Children who had been argumentative and abrasive with each other in school began to cooperate and interact positively with each other in the rural environment. From previous experience in the small group work pilot project (see Chapter 18), it had become evident that groups of four children worked well, allowing each child opportunities to talk and be listened to, which in turn allowed time to explore and extend their thinking. With more than four children, the listening time required became unsustainable for them.

It had also been noticed in school that in order to bring about change for children, it was vital to work in close partnership with parents and carers.

The project was therefore set up for four children and their primary carers to attend. These included foster, adoptive, and step parents as well as birth parents. In some cases a teaching assistant who was significant for a particular child attended.

A day at Wellie Wednesday

The children and adults were transported to what seemed to them to be like another world for six consecutive Wednesdays. The driver and another member of the team collected them from their schools and travelled fifteen miles by minibus to the outdoor activity centre where the project took place. The day started here, as attention to detail was core to the success of the project; the driver and escort had been chosen for their abilities to start the day by building optimistic expectations and by keeping conversations positive.

The location

The sessions were based mainly in a small rough field with surrounding trees. A pathway led into woodland and beyond to larger fields and the stream. Within the field there was an open shelter with a fire in the ground, two wooden tables and planks on logs for sitting together. Additional small camping chairs were used, which the children were able to move from place to place themselves. There was a tent large enough for all to sit in together near the shelter and two toilets with washing facilities.

An additional benefit was that behind the field there was an enclosed secure area with a small pond and a large caged area where red squirrels were bred for release into specified wild areas. Memorable awe and wonder moments were provided for the adults and children as together they watched the squirrels, and the children helped the wardens to feed them.

Individual secure base

Within the field four small tents were set up, one for each child, as their own safe, secure base. At the first session children were told this was their personal space, their tent was just for them. They were given a fleece blanket, a soft toy and a pillow and given time to settle in and arrange their tent. In subsequent weeks they were given individual quiet, calming activities, a range of books (fiction and non-fiction), word searches, notepad and pens. They each had a large labelled bag where all their personal belongings were kept safe from week to week. Each child made their name using pebbles; this was photographed to use as a label for their tent. This, with a photograph, was attached to their tent to give reassurance that they would return to the same safe place each week.

Social space: establishing the group

An ethos was created that promoted feelings of acceptance and respect. Children felt safe to take on new experiences and challenges. The beliefs, which were sung or spoken by the whole group at the beginning of each session, were:

> We are kind to each other.
> We follow instructions.
> We keep ourselves and each other safe.
> We look after the Wellie Wednesday environment.

These basic beliefs underpinned Wellie Wednesday and were used as reminders to maintain a sense of group cohesion and to promote positive interactions.

The wider world

The children became increasingly curious about the world around them and grew to respect and appreciate the natural environment. Being outdoors enabled them to transcend into a new world. The aim was to introduce the group to a wider world where it was hoped that they would develop a sense of awe and wonder.

> Explore nature with all our senses, feelings and emotions, for the foundation of learning is in what we love. Experience a sense of wonder so indestructible it will last throughout life.
>
> (*The Sense of Wonder*, Rachel Carson, 1965)

Occasionally, specialist visitors were invited to join a group session in order to broaden the children's experience and to support them in learning how to respond appropriately to meeting new adults, for example, not being overly familiar or highly fearful. Visitors were carefully chosen, according to the group's needs, to contribute a particular expertise, for example, orienteering, pond dipping, sheep dog training, conservation and listening to musicians.

Activities

The project was carefully planned beforehand to ensure that a range of supportive and stimulating activities were introduced to the group to encourage group identity, cooperation, responsibility and to raise feelings of self-worth. As the weeks progressed, the children and their adults were introduced to the Hope Family, a selection of models and puppets whose stories provided a vehicle to learn about thoughts, feelings and behaviour (see Figure 1.2).

A guided visualisation, the Rainbow Garden, was used to create a soothing mental image to regularly return to. Children frequently referred to using this 'safe place' to go to when they were unable to sleep. For some children, disturbing images and intrusive thoughts make any times of quiet potentially distressing. Providing imagery for a beautiful place and instruction for good things to happen in their imagination gave children a pleasurable experience. The priority for the team was to focus on the

---

The Hope Family

The Hope Family was named after 'Hope', the wonderful creature who flew from Pandora's box in the Greek myth. The story teaches that wherever there are difficulties ('Spites'), 'Hope' can always be found by those who look for her.

A family of toy turtles, tortoises and other characters were used to tell stories relating to their names, in order to create a hopeful and optimistic outlook. The endearing nature of the characters enabled children to want to identify with them. As fondness grew, the children used a number of catch phrases to help them develop the same characteristics.

- Wise Turtle taught how to calm down when feelings get uncomfortable, upset, anxious, frightened, nervous (Greenberg and Kushe 1994). Wise Turtle taught Little Turtle to 'think before you do' and 'think before you say'.
- Percy Persevere never gives up, even when it is difficult. He is helped by his friends who are called Yet, Try my Best, Practice and Can; they remind him to say 'I can't do it Yet, but if I Try my Best and Practise, soon I will be able to say I Can.'
- Patience is good at waiting when it is not her turn.
- Polly Polite uses her good manners to take turns and show respect to others.
- Princess Proud notices her 'good news' and 'getting it right' feelings.
- Iggy Ignore takes no notice of those who are not getting it right.
- Check and Change thinks about a mistake and works out how to change it to put it right.
- The Rainbow Twins live in a safe and beautiful garden and create a soothing visualisation.
- Charlie Change is a chameleon, whose motto is 'change for the better'.
- Stella is a puppet, who says 'just a minute, let me think' (Feuerstein et al. 1980) before she speaks or shouts out.

Children added their own helpers, naming new characters:

- Truthful Honesty knows the truth is always hidden inside, even when you are not telling the truth.
- Kindly Kind is thoughtful and cares about how others feel and does things willingly for others.
- Crunch the Croc learnt to use his teeth for the right purpose.

Figure 1.2 The Hope family.

Source: © Authors.

present and the future, whilst acknowledging the impact of early trauma; we believe that the Child and Adolescent Mental Health Services (CAMHS) team specialists best address the past. However, it was important to enable times of quiet to be experienced positively. During the residential camp, the children benefited from the visualisation to send them off to sleep happily and they were quick to ask for it again over the following nights (see Chapter 16).

Narrative therapy approaches were used in conversations to encourage the children to engage in problem-solving of the things they were finding difficult. They were especially helpful during follow-up visits, when each child had time to explore thinking differently about what was hampering them, using the insight and positive attitude they had gained from attending the project (see Chapter 10).

At the end of each session the team evaluated the day and identified individual targets for each child and the group focus for the following week. These were then woven into the plans for the subsequent weeks and children were encouraged to work on targets in school and at home and return with some good news to tell at breakfast time the following week. A target chart was introduced for the whole group (see Figure 1.3). Children gradually realised that adults were continually noticing and celebrating what they were getting right.

During the day, notes were made to record children's responses to the activities. Compliments were given to every child and adult and these were shared at circle time at the end of each session. During the week these were typed, printed and laminated for them to take home the following week. These built a positive picture for each person and acted as a transitional object between the project, home and school.

Figure 1.3 Getting It Right target chart.
Source: © Authors.

Ending each day

A quiet 'one minute' for reflection was incorporated into the end of the day, using a candle to focus the mind and listen to the sounds of the countryside. Everyone was invited to share a beautiful thought if they wished; this usually related to their favourite part of that day.

At the end of the day, one member of the staff joined the driver to take everyone back to their own school. This enabled them to ensure the day ended well. It was another opportunity for group members to talk together about the day and sing songs from the *Wellie Wednesday Song Book* relating to the daily activities.

Evaluation and planning

The driver and escort returned to the site for the evaluation meeting, and plans for the following week were agreed before all was tidied away and the day drew to a close. At that meeting the team considered what they had learnt about the individual children, what had worked well and what they had struggled with. This informed the target-setting and planning of activities for the following session.

Different members of the team were responsible for:

- Taking detailed notes and photographs throughout the day.
- Recording specific compliments for each person ready for the final circle.
- Typing up the notes from the day to inform the planning.
- Downloading and printing selected photographs.
- Creating individual photograph folders in preparation for printing when making the final memories books.
- Typing and printing the compliments for the whole group (staff included), laminating them ready for distribution the following week.
- Planning the week's activities to support the identified individual targets; a weekly planning sheet was distributed to all team members.
- Planning, shopping for and preparing the meals.
- Collecting and preparing the necessary resources material for each week's activities.
- Setting up for the day and safely storing all equipment at the end of the day.

Strengthening foundations

> If you always do what you've always done, you'll always get what you've always got.
>
> (Henry Ford)

The following points show how the thinking behind the project originated and evolved:

What we noticed

We considered our previous experience of group work and residential camps as an evidence base for change. It had been noted that:

- Groups of four children worked well.
- The outdoor environment enabled children to transcend into a new world.
- The camping opportunity brought about considerable change in relationships and self-esteem.

We considered levels of need

Using Abraham Maslow's pyramid structure, which demonstrates a hierarchy of needs, we noticed that the foundation underpinning needs had not been met for certain children. Until these are in place, the higher cognitive learning cannot happen.

What we recognised

To bring about change for the selected children it was vital to work in close partnership with parents and carers.

How we did what we did

Using the Concentric circles of experience diagram (see Figure 1.1):

- We created an individual safe and secure base by providing each child with their own tent.
- Significant supportive adults were available at all times.
- We then created a secure and non-threatening group space, nurturing social interactions.
- Once children felt secure within this space they were more receptive and able to engage with the opportunities available in the extended environment, 'the wider world'.

What we did

- We created an environment for learning that was different from previous experiences; experiential learning in a nurturing and enriching outdoor environment.
- We created a group ethos, which promoted feelings of acceptance and respect. Children felt safe to take on new experiences and challenges. Individual weekly targets recognised their strengths, supported areas for development and celebrated their progress.

How do we know it was successful?

The children showed progress, they:

- Applied their learning back in school.
- Showed increased confidence in themselves.
- Demonstrated the ability to interact more positively with others.
- Felt liked and valued themselves.
- Recognised the positive contribution of others.

Schools, parents and carers taking part noticed a change for the better in the children.

The fresh approach in a spacious outdoor environment, with its reassuring structure and routines, offered an opportunity for change to happen. The wide-ranging contributions of the team, supportive adults and specialist visitors, helped the children as they explored not only who they were but who they would like to become.

Reflection

What factors need to be considered when providing an educational environment that will promote kindness, compassion and understanding and awaken curiosity?

References

Carson, R. (1965). *The sense of wonder*. New York: Harper & Row.

Feuerstein, R., Feuerstein, R., Falik, L.H. and Rand, Y. (1980). *Instrumental enrichment*. Baltimore: University Park Press.

Greenberg, M. and Kushe, C. (1994). *Promoting alternative thinking skills (PATHS)*. South Deerfield: Channing-Bete.

Maslow, A.H. (1954). *Motivation and personality*. New York: Harper. Second Ed, New York: Harper (1970); Third Ed, New York: Harper (1987).

Rogers, C.R. (1983). *Freedom to learn for the 80's*. Columbus, Ohio: A. Bell and Howell Company.

Vygotsky, L. (1978). *Mind in society*. London: Harvard University Press.

Chapter 2

The valued contribution of parents, carers and other significant adults

In order for the project to achieve transferable and persistent change in the children, it was essential to invite their parents or carers to join the group (carers included step-fathers, step-mothers, adoptive parents and foster parents). In a few cases this was impossible, so another significant adult, such as a teaching assistant from the child's school, attended with the child. It was essential that each child attended with a significant, supportive adult.

Through the participation of parents and carers it was hoped that:

- They would gain an increased understanding of the importance of de-escalation strategies:
  - acknowledging feelings, 'I know you feel annoyed that...'
  - use of a calm voice, not responding to anger with anger
  - stating clear expectations, 'you need to move away from the others until you feel calm'.
- They would be able to learn the methods used by the team. Seeing team members model methods, such as appropriate ignoring and giving simple choices, would help them to encourage positive change in their children's interactions with others.
- They would gain from the opportunity to be a 'fly on the wall'; observing the team acknowledging the children's strengths and difficulties, their vulnerabilities and positively managing their challenging behaviour.
- They would begin to see their children's challenging behaviour as a means of communication and consider alternative ways of responding.
- They would see a positive impact on life at home for themselves and their children when raising self-esteem by noticing and commenting on what their children were getting right.
- They would see numerous strategies being used, which they could then use at home to defuse potentially challenging situations or behaviour. For example, they would learn to adopt the habit of interacting by encouraging and affirming.
- They would recognise their own skills and abilities to manage challenges without resorting to anger.

It was also hoped that the project would facilitate positive communication and feedback between home and school.

Meeting with parents and carers

Meetings usually took place with the parents and carers before the start of their six sessions, although the children were still introduced for the first time at the outdoor setting. This was to gather additional information and gain an insight into the adults' concerns and hopes for the future. It was considered important that the first meeting was not in school where the child was struggling. We wanted to ensure that first encounters were positive and not confused with any negative attitudes towards school.

It was recognised that some participants might feel that their own parenting skills were in question. It was therefore made clear that challenging behaviour is difficult for everyone (parents, carers, child, school) and sympathy was expressed for the difficulties that were being experienced. We recognised the adults' ambivalence, loving but being exasperated by their child, and the distress they felt when schools informed them about their child's unacceptable behaviour. We stressed that they were the person who knew their child best and as such we needed them on board to support and encourage their child. It was important to demonstrate we were there to support them in further developing their relationship with their child, so that together they could move to a more successful future.

Initial responses from the parents and carers were positive and hopeful for a changed future. Many had received ongoing feedback from schools expressing concerns regarding their child's behaviour, which resulted in anxieties about exclusion from school. It was essential that they believed change could take place and that they were willing to actively take part themselves and support their child in the project.

For many, there had been a history of interventions that had made little long-term difference, leaving them hesitant about involving themselves again. The strength of this project was that parents and carers could immediately sense it was different, in that it involved them and their child, learning new things together. The outside element, campfires and the natural environment, added an air of excitement. The result was that this project succeeded in engaging some fathers and step-fathers, unlike local parenting groups, which had a lower take-up rate with men.

Taking part in the sessions

As the sessions started the adults began to see this project as a positive alternative approach, as reflected in their comments:

- Being out in the countryside playing with other children, making things, respecting other people's feelings ... It's been a great all-round course, well worthwhile, I would recommend it to anyone as it's really worked wonders. If it were a permanent thing for kids that would be a great thing. (Father)
- She is more polite and considerate towards other people's feelings, less angry towards others. (Father)
- It offers a completely different experience away from the school environment and its associations but still with a structure and with demands being made on them. (Helper)
- I wasn't too sure what impact this would have. But the improvement I have seen has been amazing. (Mother)
- It has been a good experience to see how other people deal with children. A lot of what I have seen has been implemented at home with good results. (Father)

- I think in general the children have discovered that they can achieve a lot more both individually and as a group. (Father)
- I don't shout back anymore. I stay more relaxed. We have a bedtime routine before he gets over-tired. Now I give him a reason why he can't do something and he calms down. (Mother)
- I hope other children will get this opportunity to explore their own creativity. Children can learn so much better in a relaxed environment and I hope this scheme continues to give this experience to other children who will benefit. (Mother)

During the sessions, time was allocated for the adults to meet regularly as a group with a team leader, separate from the children. At these meetings the strategies that were being used were explained and clarified and there was an opportunity to share concerns and ask questions. Parents and carers said that they found this to be useful and reassuring. One parent asked for a list of the strategies to put on her fridge door as a reminder. Between the sessions, a member of the team was in regular telephone contact with parents and carers who were at the sessions, and also with those who had been unable to join the sessions due to work commitments or needing to care for a younger sibling.

Parents and carers were given opportunities to talk with each other away from the children; this was usually around the campfire preparing vegetables or walking across the fields, rather than in a formal meeting. They were often given tasks to perform together as a group in order to get to know each other better and build confidence. Building a waterproof shelter resulted in one parent discovering his leadership skills, gaining confidence and enjoyment that continued for the remaining sessions. Many of the parents and carers became absorbed in the activities. One father said it brought back happy memories of spending time with his grandad. Other comments about wishing they had done this sort of thing when they were children indicated the benefits they were feeling from the experiences.

Sometimes children and adults were encouraged to work in separate groups, then share their achievements with each other and acknowledge everyone's efforts with a lot of specific compliments. Not knowing what the other group were doing built up anticipation and a sense of excitement. Adults saw that building excitement ('wait and see') led to delayed gratification and greater enjoyment. For many of the children, impulsivity was a huge problem, so discovering that waiting could be enjoyable taught them a transferable skill. It was satisfying to hear one child who had had significant problems always wanting to be first saying, 'Its OK to wait when it's not my turn.'

Research has shown that there is a strong correlation between being able to delay gratification and later success in school. The 1972 Stanford Marshmallow Experiment, conducted by a psychologist, Walter Mischel, tested four-year-olds' ability to resist eating one marshmallow when left alone in order to be given two marshmallows when the experimenter returned. At twelve years of age, follow-up showed that of the 600 participants the correlations were clear: the children who could not wait were much more likely to have behavioural problems in school and at home. They struggled in stressful situations, often had trouble paying attention in class and had serious problems with their temper.

At other times, parents, carers and children worked together as partners on a task such as:

- Making eggshell heads with faces and growing cress seed hair on damp cotton wool. Parents and carers were asked to decorate an eggshell with a face, carefully keeping it hidden until it was finished. Meanwhile, the children soaked cotton wool by using a teaspoon to encourage hand–eye coordination. They transported spoonfuls of water from a beaker to the cotton wool without spilling. The adults were encouraged to remind them 'slowly and carefully'. Then they sprinkled a teaspoon of cress seeds onto the damp cotton wool. The children took turns sharing the teaspoon and watched each other. By deliberately slowing the whole process down, anticipation was built and the enjoyment of waiting and turn-taking was experienced. The egg heads were then revealed for the children to insert the cotton wool. In this way, a seemingly simple activity engaged cooperation, anticipation, coordination, patience, restraint of impulsivity and laughter when they saw the faces. By the following week the cress hair had grown, to the children's great delight.
- Making musical instruments. Children were required to communicate ideas and work with their adult to create and decorate shakers, rainsticks and drums. This was followed by the children using them to accompany a group singing session.
- Making large 'woodland faces'. These faces were made on the ground using twigs, acorns, leaves and stones in a space they had cleared of the autumn leaves. Parents and carers were surprised to find their children did 'good waiting' to see each others' ideas; it was the anticipation involved in waiting that added to the atmosphere of excitement. Spontaneous applause erupted as they looked at the finished faces of each pair.

Sometimes children were given a task to do for their parent or carer:

- Filling a pancake and making burgers. At these times it was the adults who had to do 'good waiting' and the children had to keep from excitedly calling out what the surprise was to be. Children calling out answers often caused irritation in school, so learning restraint in a fun way taught them that they could resist the temptation to call out, another transferable skill. For example, a child told us:

I knew an answer in maths but I didn't call out. I got it wrong though!

- Sharing. The sharing of the fruit plate at snack time involved chopping and handing round a plate of fruit. This enabled parents and carers to see how children could learn to share and gain enjoyment from it. The peeling, cutting and arranging of fruit on the plate, then taking turns to choose pieces, all made for a special cooperative and social time. Children found they were happy to share. Adults realised they could use this idea at home to avoid sibling squabbles over sweets or biscuits. By introducing sharing and slowing the process down, they could make more of a social event of treats and snacks. Social skills were also learnt, for example, 'Does anyone else want the last piece of banana?', ensuring everyone has had some, the person passing the plate waiting until last. One mother told us at a follow-up meeting that she used the shared fruit plate as an after school snack and a good time for her sons to get on well together.

Ongoing observations

Parents and carers were encouraged to objectively observe their own child and not feel threatened, embarrassed or criticised. What they noticed about the children and themselves was:

- Surprise at their child's positive response to the outdoor environment and the agreed ground rules. One mother said that she was amazed that her son had been outside all day, normally he did not want to go out.
- They welcomed the opportunity to enjoy their child's company in a way that they had not experienced before.
- They observed strengths in their child of which they were not previously aware.
- Some recognised how little time they had been able to spend alone with their child due to demands of younger and older siblings.
- They realised that other parents and carers often had the same anxieties and challenges as themselves.
- Some felt emotional as they began to recognise and express their own anxieties and share them within a supportive group.
- Some gained reassurance by sharing common issues and strategies with each other; growing in confidence as they recognised their own strengths.
- Most realised how unfamiliar if felt to receive compliments and acknowledge their own strengths and abilities.
- All recognised the positive effect when noticing and commenting on others getting it right. They saw the benefits and recognised the importance as they developed their 'language of compliments'.

Reflection

How can we offer opportunities for parents and carers to be part of successful change in their child's learning? How can the importance of focusing on small things that the child is getting right be communicated to parents and carers?

Part II

Can I be included?

Case studies, including impact on family and school, strategies used, changes noticed and key questions raised

Chapter 3

Yasmin
Daring to join in

At Wellie Wednesday I noticed more that people liked me. I didn't know before.
(Yasmin)

Referral concerns from school and home

- Fluctuation between shyness and defiant outbursts.
- She frequently left the classroom complaining in a whining voice and often became tearful.
- She was especially distressed during maths.
- Yasmin would only eat a very restricted diet, mostly of sweet items or crisps.

Yasmin's strengths as seen by the team

- Yasmin is an able child, capable of good work.
- She is able to make connections, linking past experience with new knowledge.
- She is good at reading.
- She loves art activities.
- She has a good general knowledge.
- She has a very good memory.

Understanding and making sense of the concerns raised

Yasmin had been inadvertently allowed to become powerful in deciding what she would and would not do or eat. Fear of Yasmin's tears or tantrums had prevented adults from taking control. Yasmin's high anxiety resulted in her presenting herself as a shy and tearful child who lacked confidence.

Yasmin's perceived needs and individual targets

- To reduce her fearfulness particularly around known triggers such as food and maths.
- To accept the need to follow instructions.
- To recognise her own strengths and abilities.
- To learn about persistence and to feel successful through the experience of not giving up.

- To communicate her thoughts and feelings clearly.
- To enjoy interacting with others.
- To transfer her new-found skills and self-belief to dealing with challenging situations in school.

Strategies used by the team to support Yasmin's needs

Using the target chart to recognise her own successes

The target chart, as previously mentioned, was used to record successes. The targets were linked to songs, stories and sayings to help familiarise and embed them in the children's thinking and behaviour. From the start, Yasmin was particularly good at recognising the efforts of others. Her face lit up when it was time to add ticks to the chart and she was quick to identify which targets had been achieved by herself and others. The chart became a personal incentive for her as she purposefully incorporated these targets into her thinking, which then changed her behaviour.

> The target chart served as a visual reminder of behaviour that was expected and therefore praised. Some adults were surprised that what was assumed to be 'normal good behaviour' should be remarked upon as praiseworthy. However, at Wellie Wednesday, the aim was to reshape negative behaviour patterns by praising every move in the right direction. Praise was given for 'good sitting' before any expectation of starting work had even been mentioned. Similarly with 'good listening', 'good thinking' (when an idea is forthcoming), 'good speaking' (when a question has been answered in a clear voice), 'good waiting' (when it has not been their turn, or if others are off task), 'good following instructions' (when they have done as asked, i.e. come to the desk, got their books out).
>
> These targets can be used to praise and encourage behaviour that is leading towards good working. In this way, a previously unsuccessful and disruptive child starts to feel a sense of achievement and gains the confidence to attempt more challenging targets. Use of the target chart encourages behaviour that soon becomes automatic. As the on-task behaviour starts to become the norm, the need for ticks on the chart diminishes. There are times when the chart becomes less of a focus. However, whenever a group shows signs of struggling or restlessness then returning to the chart and allowing the group to suggest which targets deserve ticks is usually enough to re-settle the group. It is also an opportunity for individuals to praise each other and recall what they have noticed others getting right, thus encouraging collaboration. More challenging targets are added as time goes on.

Praise and attention focused on positive behaviour

The adults modelled the importance of explicit praise by noticing specific positive actions, however tiny: 'Well done Yasmin for picking up that piece of paper so it didn't blow away', 'I noticed you didn't give up when it was hard work carrying that chair to our circle. That was good persevering.' Ignoring her low-level undesirable behaviour, for example, whining voice, complaining and a negative attitude was countered by making a positive comment to a nearby child, thereby highlighting the desired behaviour: 'I like your good speaking when you answered that question.' Yasmin watched with concentration, noticing where the attention was focused, consequently, she adapted her interactions.

Use of compliments

Every session ended with a formal circle time featuring compliments. Each person, including the adults, was reminded of a specific good thing that had been noticed about them. Some teachers expressed concern that it might be used as a time to flatter a special friend whilst overlooking a less popular peer. This was always structured so the focus moved round the circle, ensuring one person did not receive lots of compliments whilst another had none. Once modelled, we found children were soon able to give their own compliments. We found the children became observant, generous and honest. Noticing what others are getting right taught the children to recognise positive qualities and kind words and actions in others; this inspired Yasmin and the other children to develop these qualities in themselves.

Children may be used to adults praising children but giving and receiving compliments from each other had a very powerful effect as noted by some of the children's comments:

> I had never thought of saying kind things to other people before.

> I liked it when you gave Laura (child's teaching assistant) a compliment, I didn't think she would get one because she is a grown-up.

It is the act of saying that seems to make the difference. Speaking a compliment to another person is an interactive experience leading to positive reciprocal feelings. The child who had not thought of saying kind things had certainly been told in school to be kind, but being told to be kind and doing it yourself are very different experiences in terms of the positive effect engendered. Being kind to others makes sense when you find it makes you feel good too.

Yasmin's compliment at the first week's final circle was:

> Yasmin, you were very helpful when you showed the other children how to roll up their tent door.

She had been encouraged to show the others how to do this having mastered it herself. So she ended the week thinking less about what she couldn't do and more about her positive interactions with others.

Developing a sense of fun, fostering enjoyment

Yasmin and her father were able to enjoy joint success by carrying out cooperative activities. An example was making mobiles using wood that needed holes drilled, sanding and decorating, then tying the pieces together, another novel activity for the group. Yasmin's father was asked to oversee each child having a turn making a hole using a brace and bit. Yasmin was visibly excited about her father's responsible role and loved her turn with him. She had no difficulty willingly following his instructions for this task.

Games and stories were used to explain different ways of interacting. For example, 'Share a Smile' was used as a game to demonstrate that the way we behave influences how others treat us. In the circle, one person started by smiling at another, who passed it on, and so on. Yasmin enjoyed this and was pleased when she found that at school when she smiled at people in the corridors they smiled back. 'Having a go' was more easily encouraged for Yasmin through taking part in games. It then became less anxiety-raising for her when she was asked to undertake tasks in school. However small or undemanding the task, she would be praised for having a go: 'Well done Yasmin, that was a good try.' Little attention was paid to how well it was achieved by comparison with the effort made.

Once she felt that joining in, having a go and trying were possible for her, she stopped retreating to the fringes of the group and started to take a more active role. Success in small things quickly led to a more confident attitude and transferred to school where she remained in class and got on with her work.

Use of narrative approaches to address difficulties

When discussing how Yasmin could keep crying out, it was suggested that she could 'Try not Cry' (see Chapter 10). This linked with Percy Persevere the tortoise (see Chapter 1), who kept going even when things were difficult, and his tortoise helpers, Yet, Try My Best, Practise and Can, whose catchphrase was:

I can't do it YET

but if I TRY MY BEST

and PRACTISE

soon I will be able to say I CAN

This gave her an alternative focus with which to manage her fearfulness. Yasmin's fears resulted in her crying. Our aim was not to stop her crying but to help her to overcome the fearfulness and remove the need for crying. When Yasmin had initially been scared to go into the woods she was encouraged to hold the Percy Persevere tortoise, whose story tells of not giving up, so she found the confidence to have a go even though it felt difficult. She managed to overcome her initial apprehension and found that she enjoyed the woodland activities. From then on, she would sometimes collect Percy to take with her to hold if she thought something was going to be difficult for her.

Eating a communal meal in a social setting

Yasmin's first mealtime was difficult. She had brought a backpack with her lunch box and all her favourite treats: crisps, juice, chocolate and a sandwich. Her father had allowed this, so great was his fear of her response to being asked to eat other foods, and publicly, in a new situation. It was important to set the boundaries clearly for Yasmin so the following week she would not put her father in a difficult position again. It was explained that she might make others feel left out if she ate her things while they had not been allowed to bring food of their own choice. Her father was reassured she would not suffer if she chose not to eat any of the other foods on offer. The light-hearted conversation and laughter drew her back to the group where she saw other children experiencing great delight at the meal cooked over the fire. She observed all the food-related interactions with interest from the sidelines. The following week a decision was made to entice her with a hands-on food preparation session. Savoury pancakes were chosen. Children had fun watching them cook, then filling them. The children chopped and mixed fillings, then their parent or carer chose which fillings they would like. This was a memory test as each child had to go to their adult and list the options, then remember what had been requested. They filled and rolled the pancakes and served them to their adult. They enjoyed watching, interacting and tasting new foods. Yasmin had plenty of time to observe the others and to serve her father before it was time for her to eat. In a casual way she was asked, just as the others had been, what filling she was going to try. No-one made any reference to knowing she only ate very few foods. She gave one look towards her father to see if he was going to bail her out then tentatively rolled some ham into a pancake and sat down. No-one paid any attention, giving her time to experiment, then she joined the pleadings for more pancakes from the cook. Soon she was revelling in asking again for more and the pancake-making continued. To her delight, one of the team said: 'I'm going to call you the Pancake Princess now.' Involving her in the preparation and serving of food had helped her to feel less threatened by unfamiliar foods. Reminding her of her new title helped her to continue to experiment when new foods were added to the menu.

Use of limited choice to prevent opting out or refusal

It is easier for a child to respond to instructions when given a specific choice, for example: 'You need to be in the classroom now. Are you going to walk in on your own or do you need me to come with you?' Concentrating on making the choice serves to distract from thoughts of refusal and gives them a sense of autonomy in that they are saying what they will do. When given two alternatives, Yasmin was usually able to make a choice rather than opting out. For instance, when Yasmin was nervous about jumping into a big pile of leaves, she was asked: 'Do you want to have a go by yourself or would you like to do it with one of the others?' She chose to jump with Annabelle and emerged happily from the leaves ready for another turn, this time on her own.

Impact on the family

For Yasmin's father, Wellie Wednesday was an opportunity to see his child in a different light. He was able to experience different ways of interacting with her. He no longer felt the need to appease her at all costs in order to avoid the risk of an outburst. A new calmer and more contented Yasmin emerged as her father took back control as he found how well she responded to clear instructions, praise and higher expectations. They also discovered how to work together and relished their new-found enjoyment of calmer, more fun-filled times. Yasmin particularly enjoyed being given responsibilities and finding that she was trusted. Her father's comments showed how much had changed for them:

> Wellie Wednesday has had a good effect on me, seeing she can do things without me constantly having to supervise her.

> It has been a good experience to see how other people deal with children.

> A lot of what I have seen has been implemented at home with good results.

Changes noticed in Yasmin

Yasmin said she was proud that 'I help by putting the bins out, I help Dad with the washing up, I tidy up … oh and I also put stuff in the tumble dryer.' She was excited to tell us that her grandmother had bought two pop-up tents for indoor use so she and her sister have their own special place now. She said she kept her Wellie Wednesday book in her tent and came home from school to give herself ticks on the target chart page for things she had got right that day. She added she was running out of space on it! Well-deserved extra copies were immediately sent. It was another example of how each child internalises what they need and makes it their own.

The Boxall profile (Bennathan and Boxall 1998) was used to identify areas of need and to enable developmental progress to be monitored. Yasmin's improvements were confirmed by this method when it was administered at the end of the school year. It showed as completely normal with no areas of concern, reassuring us that the enormous improvement seen after the project had been maintained back in school. Her own realisation of the change she had experienced was summed up when she told us the last week:

> I'm more helpful, really helpful and kind at school. I brought in sweets, I wanted to thank everyone for being kind to me. At Wellie Wednesday I noticed more that people liked me. I didn't know before.

Transferring learning into school

In school, Yasmin was able to remember occasions when she had overcome her fearfulness. She transferred the feelings of reassurance by thinking of Percy Persevere and reciting the phrases that had helped her. When talking about maths at a follow-up meeting, she said: 'I have turned Cry into Try.' She had also internalised the message of the other tortoises and their catchphrase. It was not long before she was able to tell us her good news, indicating that her fear of maths was gone. She told us: 'I remember the Try Turtles and say I can't do it YET, but if I Try My Best then I CAN and it works.'

The set of small plastic tortoises charmed and gave strength to many hesitant and fearful children for whom the risk of failing had prevented them from attempting many tasks. One child in school adopted the 'Can' tortoise as his special helper so when he started to panic, instead of storming away from his desk, he was encouraged to go and collect Can and bring her to sit on his desk. The action of allowing him to move away in an acceptable way gave him a few moments of physical distraction, then as he held the little tortoise, the positive feelings that she elicited calmed him enough to have a 'Try'. Permission to 'Try My Best' seems to tap into a very different mindset to that of needing to get something right. The latter produces high anxiety and even triggers fight, flight or freeze responses, thereby closing down frontal lobe activity (Hannaford 1995). The former, by not triggering this pathway, enables the frontal cortex to engage in cognitive functioning and as thinking occurs, makes 'I can' moments more likely.

At a follow-up school visit, when asked again how maths was going, Yasmin said it was good. When asked how she managed to make it good, she said: 'When I do my homework I do all the hard ones first then I get left with the easy ones.' Not only had she lost her fear of maths but she had developed her own successful strategy for tackling it. It was a big change from tearful refusal to looking for the hardest sums first.

Yasmin was rebuilding her own self-image to one of being a successful learner. She had told no-one in school what she was doing to help herself, i.e. using her target chart and doing the hard sums first, but her behaviour and learning were being noticed. Her headteacher said: 'Yasmin is a changed child. She used to be a non-participator, now she initiates ideas.' Her confidence was such that she stood up in front of the whole school at assembly to share with them what Wellie Wednesday had been all about.

Teachers now felt able to take her on school outings and her first was to sing to residents in a local care home for the elderly. She also contributed a beautiful piece of artwork to an exhibition at a local arts centre and she happily stood beside it talking to visitors about her painting.

Yasmin was reaping the many benefits of her changed outlook on life. She transferred to her next school the following year without difficulty and follow-up information continues to be very positive, with the Boxall profile endorsing this by continuing to show no concerns.

Key strategies used

- Using the target chart to recognise her own successes.
- Praise and attention focused on positive behaviour.

- The use of compliments.
- Developing a sense of fun and fostering a sense of enjoyment.
- Interactive sociable mealtime: the 'Pancake Princess'.
- The use of narrative conversations to address difficulties.
- Offering a limited choice.

Reflection

When a child presents as shy, tearful and lacking in confidence, how can we ensure their true potential is realised? What is the link between giving a child too much choice or too many decisions to make and anxiety-driven behaviour, such as tantrums, tears and anxiety?

References

Bennathan, M. and Boxall, M. (1998). *The Boxall profile: A guide to effective intervention in the education of pupils with emotional and behavioural difficulties; Handbook for teachers.* Nurture Group Consortium; Association of Workers for Children with Emotional and Behavioural Difficulties. Maidstone: AWCEBD.

Hannaford, C. (1995). *Smart moves: Why learning is not all in your head.* Georgia: Great Ocean Publishers.

Chapter 4

Amber

Picking up speed

At a follow-up meeting in school Amber said: 'I still use "check and change". I said to myself, "Shall I hit my brother or shall I not?" In the end, I didn't.'

Referral concerns from school and home

- Amber tells lies, she seems to have no sense of the truth; she seems unable to distinguish fact from fantasy.
- Amber steals; she will take small items from other children and the classroom, these are not always items she even really wants, for example, paper clips from the class teacher desk, pieces of Lego, Blu-Tack.
- Amber takes food from other children's lunch boxes.
- She will use the diversion of going to the toilet to avoid work and see what is happening outside the classroom.
- She see-saws between being first to grab equipment, or hanging back and being deliberately slow, requiring chasing up or further instruction.
- She appears to derive satisfaction from disrupting friendship groups. She is very quick to stir up dissension, then as soon as there are signs of upset she will run off and claim not to have been there.
- Amber watches others all the time, adults and peers, then spots opportunities to target weaker children with unkind comments and sometimes actions, for example, pinching, taking something they were playing with.
- She is drawn like a magnet to arguments and angry outbursts of other children, always first on the scene with a tendency to jump in and take over with an opinion of what had happened, despite not having been there at the time of the incident.
- Amber avoids any sort of reflection about her behaviour, she seems only able to use blame or denial.

Amber's strengths as seen by the team

- She is quick on the uptake.
- She is alert.
- She is enthusiastic.
- She enjoys being helpful to adults.
- She is physically able.

Understanding and making sense of concerns raised

The long list of concerns from school indicated to the team that Amber was a little girl who had learnt to gain attention in many anti-social ways. She had also found ways to create disturbance and discord, creating an energy level that gave her a buzz of satisfaction.

However, the frequency with which she was unkind to herself and towards others indicated a child who suffered from a negative self-image with all of its associated uncomfortable feelings. She rarely smiled, except when running off after teasing another child or when watching others arguing.

Taking food and other items can sometimes be seen as a way that a child may be trying to fill emotional rather than physical gaps. They believe that posessing what others have will make them feel better. By being unkind to others, Amber was seemingly trying to pass on her uncomfortable feelings in order to try to get rid of them. Perhaps her experiences were primarily of put-downs and punishments, and attention only being available when her challenging behaviour demanded it.

In school, her 'slow coach' behaviour ensured individual attention. At home, her ploy of eating her meals slowly prolonged her mother's focus. Both were successful strategies for gaining attention.

Amber's perceived needs and individual targets

- To develop a positive self-image.
- To understand everyone has comfortable and uncomfortable feelings and to learn to distinguish between them.
- To build her repertoire of positive affect and its vocabulary.
- To provide opportunities for her to receive positive reinforcement for kind, helpful, thoughtful behaviour.
- To teach her ways to relax with a calming visualisation, replacing negative thoughts with relaxing breathing and positive sayings.
- To develop kindness towards herself and others.
- To develop an understanding of fact and fantasy.

Strategies used by the team to support Amber's needs

Specific praise

The team responded with specific praise quickly when Amber was on task, behaving appropriately or acting calmly, at the same time being careful of giving no positive attention when she was off task. It was rapidly apparent how easily Amber could engage adults in conversation at times when another adult had given her an instruction. She also tried using her 'going to the toilet' strategy to remove herself from the group in order to wander off in the direction of the toilets, but only until she could spot another adult to go to and charmingly offer to help with whatever they were doing. The team were briefed to start any engagement with Amber by saying, 'I will talk to you later but where are you supposed to be now?'

Good ignoring

Amber's low-level disruptions were responded to by turning attention to another child and praising them for 'good ignoring', i.e. not joining in, this would quickly bring Amber back to being on task to get her share of praise too. As soon as any child who had left the group rejoined or started a previously refused task, it was vital to give praise quickly, for example, 'good sitting' or 'good choice to join in'. If a task was going to prove difficult for a child, then moving in to offer support quickly showed them that recognising they needed help prevented the need to avoid the task. In these ways, Amber learnt to gain attention positively.

De-escalation

Children are drawn to energised situations; Amber had certainly learnt to find them. She was always first to the scene of any playground disagreement, quickly fuelling it by joining in, taking sides and adding inflammatory comments. She was also able to create discord herself through telling tales, disrupting friendships, spreading untrue stories and deliberately spoiling games, for example, by taking a vital part of the equipment.

The team knew to react with very low energy responses when they were faced with Amber's negative behaviour. Previously, adults, both at home and at school, had inadvertently fed Amber's desire for dramatic attention by reacting with irritation, speaking angrily or trying to punish. When Amber succeeded in infuriating, irritating or frustrating others the adults learnt to manage this by remembering that: 'All feelings are OK but behaviour can be OK or not OK.' Adults will at times feel frustrated and annoyed but any behaviour that hints of desperation only serves to feed the child's undesirable behaviour. Acting calmly despite feeling otherwise is an essential skill to master: using cognitive thoughts to override uncomfortable feelings is a known stress-reducing strategy. The groups learnt this as 'helpful and unhelpful thinking' tactics. As Amber was no longer to gain attention in her familiar ways she did still need highly energised experiences but now they were gained through enjoying playfulness and fun with the adults, i.e. energised positive interactions as an alternative way of receiving and giving attention.

'Keeping Trouble out': Externalising the problem by using narrative approaches

Two displays of Amber's behaviour caused particular difficulty, her deliberate slowness and her stealing. A combination of using a narrative approach to keeping Trouble out, the use of metaphor in storytelling and explicit teaching about thinking, feelings and behaviour were all part of the group experience designed to address unhelpful behaviour.

When faced with problem behaviour we always found the best starting point for enabling change was to ask the child what they thought their particular difficulty meant. 'What does stealing/lying/dishonesty/the truth mean?'

Words are often used with an assumption that children understand their meaning. A child's own definition or explanation usually sheds light on their perception of the difficulty. This would then be followed by 'So X [behaviour] is being a bit tricky and getting you into trouble is it?' 'How would it be if X wasn't around?' The child is then able to explore the benefits of ridding themselves of the problem. They are also exposed to the reality of how the behaviour is impacting on their lives, turning round their previously held notion that by causing trouble it somehow gains them the benefit of seeming to win a power or attention battle.

Responses elicited from the child are then repeated back in a spirit of curiosity. 'So are you saying that if X didn't happen then friends would like you better?' or 'So if X wasn't around Mum wouldn't get cross with you?' As the problem is externalised, so the child experiences, perhaps for the first time, feeling themselves as separate from the behaviour. The problem is even personified, its characteristics identified and how it works to cause trouble. Children usually enjoy this process, it brings humour and playfulness to what has always been a problematic subject to talk about. Frequently, they are surprised by what they learn. One boy exclaimed: 'I never knew that before I said it.' Having described the problem behaviour and named it (for example, 'Trouble'), as fully as possible the next idea pondered is 'Sounds as if Trouble is stopping you having a good time and getting it right, that doesn't seem fair', followed by 'I wonder how you could keep Trouble out?' Children then fathom their own responses and often find ingenious solutions. Feeling empowered to 'keep Trouble out' using their own idea can bring some startling and rapid results (see Chapter 10).

When Amber was asked how she could keep 'Slowness' out she found her own imaginative way to solve her 'always being last' problem. 'I am a snail but I am going to be a cheetah now, they are the fastest animal.' 'I will say to myself every time don't be a snail be a cheetah.' The adults reinforced her idea by failing to engage in conversation with her when she was slow. If a reminder was needed, a quizzical look and 'cheetah or snail?' said in a friendly questioning tone usually brought about the right response.

Subsequently at good news time, when asked to tell us of a time when she had been a cheetah during the week she replied 'I'm getting really fast for eating my tea, I used to be really slow but now I don't be.' Her mum looked proud and said it was true that she eats up well now.

Later on at a follow-up meeting in school she explained:

> Being a cheetah means being fast at doing something: I'm getting it right, not a snail but a cheetah. I say I CAN do it and I say I CAN get it right.

Honesty: Taking things

Amber's stealing was not addressed overtly, instead she was given the positive experiences of what trust, honesty and truth mean allowing meaning and metaphor to be internalised. Stories and a character named Truthful Honesty were used to explore ideas about truth and the consequences of dishonesty. At the same time as she was given opportunities to develop positive behaviour so that she experienced the associated feelings of joy, pleasure, social connection and feeling valued. These were the feelings we wanted to create in her to hopefully take the place that she had previously tried to fill in other ways, maybe even by taking other people's possessions. Her own words later supported this view when, without mention of her stealing, she said she used to take things when she was sad but now she is a happy girl she doesn't feel like taking things.

Telling the truth: Fact and fantasy

For some children what the truth means has not necessarily been modelled to them so basic unemotive teaching needs to establish what is meant by the difficult concept behind the all too familiar words 'telling the truth'. As a precursor to learning about truth the teaching sessions about the brain incorporated information on using the imagination and then comparing ideas from imaginative thinking to facts and factual recall. Games were used where everyone makes three statements, two of which are true and one is from their imagination, then the others have to guess which is which. Humour and fun add to the activity and so a serious lesson is learnt in a playful manner. From then on, what is said can be queried with: 'Is that true or imagined?'

As Amber's familiarity with using her imagination grew it was possible to explore further what telling the truth meant. In Amber's case she was:

- Able to establish that the truth meant it really happened but that in our imaginations fantasies or make believe can be created.
- Given times during which she was encouraged to make things up in a creative way by using her imagination. So she learnt that imaginative thinking had its place but was a separate type of thinking from recounting factual events.
- Able to explore the idea that sometimes her answers were saying what she wished or wanted to be true (see reference to magical thinking, Chapter 7).

Adults were encouraged to ask her if what she had said was true or if it was what she would like to be true. As Amber was supported to think more accurately about her responses, and as she instead of Amber was able to practise separating fact from fantasy, the instances of her lying diminished and she became better able to acknowledge when she had lied.

A story based on Fragile Eggs by David Straker (available online) communicated very clearly the relationship between trust and truth. Amber studied with interest a tiny wooden tortoise with an openwork carved shell that revealed a smaller tortoise inside. She came to the realisation that, 'The truth is always hidden inside you, even if other people don't know you have lied.' Amber named this tortoise 'Truthful Honesty'.

Not all children come to school with a firm foundation in trust and openness. Many children, from a very early age, experience punishment whenever they have been perceived to have done something wrong. These children are much more likely to develop the strategies of lying and blaming others in order to avoid punishment. By the time they reach school, avoidance of the truth can then be an entrenched behaviour. Consequences in school will often serve to confirm that getting better at blaming others and lying more convincingly is what is needed. In these cases, a calm supportive instruction for reparation of the misdeed may be the best solution, for example, 'I'll help you write a note to the lunchtime supervisers who you were rude to.' Or, 'I will help you but now we need to pick up the things you threw.' This allows for praise to follow, for example, 'Well done for helping clear up the mess you made.' For a child who does not yet understand 'sorry' or feel empathy, this is often more instructive than insisting on an insincere apology. With support for taking these steps the child learns through experience how to take responsibility for their actions. Once accepting responsibility and the consequences then it becomes possible to avoid making the same mistake in the future.

Expressing feelings: 'I feel ... because ...'

The groups were taught to use 'I feel ... because ...' language when they were getting annoyed, upset or cross with another person. Accusing and telling tales both activate defensive behaviour in the recipient resulting in exacerbating confrontational reactions. However, when a feeling is mentioned first and then the problem, a different response is usually triggered. Through using this approach, Amber started to respond differently. She was much more willing to stay around to problem-solve when she heard people say they felt upset or unhappy and then described their problem.

It was as if her interest had been aroused, when, initially with adult support, the problem was described 'We both want to play with the same thing' and then a question was posed, 'What can be done about that then? How are you going to sort it out?' and she would engage with finding a satisfactory solution.

When children are given the responsibility, without adults making the decision for them, and thereby seeming to take sides, children come up with solutions that work for them. 'I feel ... because ...' describes the difficulty rather than starting by accusing the other person: 'You did/said ...'. The group also learnt that 'a problem shared is a problem halved', so praise for problem-solving took the place of emotive tale telling, accusations and arguments.

The importance of smiling

Amber had been described as frequently frowning, scowling and pouting. These facial expressions are linked to uncomfortable feelings that are not conducive to a constructive state of mind, let alone one where successful learning can be achieved. She needed to experience playful smiles and laughter-eliciting activities to promote the feelings of well-being that are helpful in reaching a state of readiness to learn.

Some adults seem to make the assumption that sarcasm, jokey leg pulling, the use of derogatory names and language were harmless fun. Children too will often be heard saying 'I was only joking' and 'I didn't really mean it'; these are frequently heard playground comments. A culture of disrespectful banter can be harmful. Children's brains are continuing to develop and to be regularly receiving negative messages will be anxiety-raising. In turn, persistent anxiety is known to be detrimental because it further activates the neurological wiring of the brain's threat system. The brain is alert to potential danger but if repeatedly triggered, albeit by words and actions used in jest, then relaxation and calmness become less and less accessible states of mind.

Amber enjoyed learning the smile games. Share a smile this involved passing a smile around the circle. Each person in turn smiled at another. It was quickly realised that smiling is contagious and Amber's smile began to form in response to others. The Smile Game helped to emphasise the importance and effect of smiling. Amber started making eye contact , smiling and finding that it generated another smile.

Find a smila: a smiley disc was threaded onto a circle of string and passed around under each person's hands as the song was sung. One person stood in the centre and at the end of the song had to identify who was smiling as they were the person now holding the disc.

Pass the smile song
(to the tune of "London bridge is falling down")

> Pass the smile
> Around and round, round and round
> round and round
>
> Pass the smile
> Around and round,
> Whose turn is it?

The significance of the smile

This simple 'smiling practice' was based in the theory that to smile is a first way of building social bonds. From infancy, smiling is a way to communicate first with parents, then with others. Smiling and frowning do not occur together so when we meet with children for whom the frown seems to be their default setting it is important to change this. Smiling is universally recognised, unlike language and cultural customs. Smiling is known to release endorphins in the brain and studies have shown that this happens with a false smile as well as with the involuntary true ones (Laird 1974). So creating games, rhymes and opportunities to elicit smiling was an important part of each day.

Another smile was shared:

One smile or two?

A smile is such a happy thing
It wrinkles up your face
And when it's gone you'll never find its secret hiding place.
But far more wonderful than that is what a smile can do.
You smile at him
He smiles at you
And so one a smile makes two.

Lunchtime joke- and riddle-telling became a favourite time of the day and had the added bonuses of children committing them to memory during the week as well as having to contain their excitement until the correct time in the day. Being able to delay gratification, as mentioned previously, is a known indicator of future success so it was important that naturally impulsive children learnt to restrain themselves. The payoff therefore had to be sufficiently rewarding and an audience laughing with them was certainly a sought after experience! It was a good way to encourage appropriate affect modulation, for example, many children become over excited very easily, laughter turning to uncontrolled hilarity. Imposing some structure helped to create a fun occasion without it getting out of hand.

We are kind to each other

Amber had difficulty being kind; it was essential that this was addressed. Other children at Wellie Wednesday also experienced this difficulty and for this reason our group ethos was: 'We are kind to each other and we keep ourselves and each other safe.' Derived from knowing that safety and kindness are two of the most basic human needs, they were therefore at the core of how the group functioned. We found they were quickly absorbed into the children's thinking and became part of their language, well-illustrated by one child, who told us: 'I've been kind to my teacher by working hard.' Questions such as 'Is that being kind?', 'Can you use kind words to say that?', 'Is that keeping yourself safe?' became ways to help a child reflect on their unkind words and actions.

The brain is programmed to respond to kindness from birth. We found that explicit and continuing reference to kindness did have a soothing effect on the children. It was indeed as if they instinctively knew it was what they needed. Learning how to elicit kindness from others then became available to them. Using compliments to highlight these feelings and behaviour helped the children broaden their repertoire of positive ways to interact. Yasmin told us: 'I like giving compliments, I had never thought of saying nice things to other people before.' She had needed the experience of kindness in action through the giving of compliments to discover how it felt.

Our culture of compliments was a formal reminder of each member's contribution to the day. It was not surprising to find how important these were to the adults as well as the children. Initially, many parents found it difficult to think of anything they felt proud of, the good news time was difficult at first but gradually the successes were being noticed and we were hearing how parents were involving the children and building up family teamwork.

Quotes from parents:

I made really good gravy with the roast dinner this week, everyone said so.

I let the kids have paints, I put the table outside so I wouldn't mind the mess, they had real fun.

I gave myself 'time out' when I was getting stressed with them, they thought it was really funny we all ended up laughing.

I took the kids to the park, we looked for bugs.

I let Sam help me get the tea (I usually think it's easier to do it myself).

Self-soothing techniques: 7/11 breathing and guided visualisation

To help strengthen Amber's self-soothing system, she was taught a relaxation breathing method: '7/11 breathing'. This involved learning to control the breath by inhaling to the count of seven and exhaling to the count of eleven. Another soothing strategy was a guided visualisation: the Rainbow Garden. This visualisation creates a mental image of a place where the Rainbow Twins (see Chapter 16) are always waiting, always kind, and always keep the garden a safe place to visit. Amber learnt to imagine her own safe place within the garden where she could look out and experience something special, just for her. She enjoyed this and was able to gradually increase the time spent in this quiet meditative experience. Many children over the years have told us that they continue to use this exercise to help get to sleep.

When my brother is nasty to me I go upstairs and under my duvet to the Rainbow Garden.

Impact on family

For Amber's mother and step-father, being involved in learning with Amber was a different experience. As Amber and her parents enjoyed being part of a team, experiencing new things together and encouraging each other, Amber became visibly more relaxed. Her parents felt less need to admonish and punish as they learnt how to praise and give clear instructions. Together they learnt new ways of communicating and lessons using a model brain were as new to them as to Amber. Learning that our brains seek and recognise kindness was important and that as kindness is experienced and the benefits are felt so it becomes easier to be kind to oneself and to others.

The smiling, speedier Amber was easier for her mother to manage and together they spent more time having fun and less time arguing. The family took up the activities they had been shown, and bug hunting at the park, collage making and leaf identifying all started to happen at home. Trips to the library for nature books, to the park, and weekly swimming all brought the family together. Sibling relationships improved and Amber enjoyed her role as responsible older sister. One week, she was delighted to tell us her good news was that she had bought playing cards at a Bring and Buy sale, and she and her mum had played cards after the younger children were in bed.

> I do my brother's jigsaw with him then Mum does mine with me.

Changes noticed in Amber

As Amber's ability to talk about her feelings increased, so her need to communicate through her anti-social behaviour decreased. Her observations of herself and others changed too. Now she looked for others being happy instead of noticing the negatives and rushing to tell tales. She told us:

- The good news is Eddie (step-father) has a smiley face now.
- I keep my hands to myself so I have kind hands now.
- I can keep things safe, not take things.

Amber was also able to reflect on her own behaviour. When asked at a follow-up meeting what had changed for her, she replied that before:

> I was sad and wanted to take things. Now I am a happy laughing girl I don't take things.

Transferring learning into school

Amber became much more ready to admit her mistakes. She was able to learn that it is possible to 'check and change', i.e. see a mistake and put it right. This, in combination with 'Think before you do', enabled Amber to feel less frantic and more in control of deciding what to do, instead of reacting impulsively.

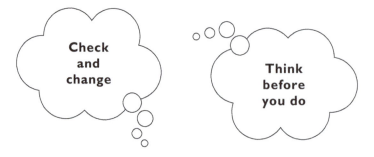

At a follow-up meeting in school she said: 'I still use check and change. I said to myself, shall I hit my brother or shall I not? In the end I didn't.' She then drew a picture of her brain and in it were some maths sums, and she wanted written on it: 'When I do handwriting I check and change to draw the letters right.' She wanted its title to be 'Inside my brain' followed by the words, 'I think hard. It (my brain) gets ready to say the right answer.'

Key strategies used

- Ignoring low-level negative behaviour.
- Low energy responses to negative behaviour, i.e. calm low voice, few words.
- Positive playful interactions with adults as well as peers.
- 'I feel ... because ...' language used to express to her the effect of her actions on others.
- giving praise for sharing a problem: 'a problem shared is a problem halved.'
- Keeping Trouble out.
- Fact and fantasy.
- The smile games.
- We keep ourselves and each other safe.
- Self-soothing strategies.
- Think before you do or say.
- Check and change.

Reflection

For troubled children, or those with poor language skills, how do we ensure that they understand what telling the truth really means?

Reference

Laird, J.D. (1974). Self-attribution of emotion: The effects of expressive behavior on the quality of emotional experience. *Journal of Personality and Social Psychology* 29(4): 475–486.

Chapter 5

Ashley

Safe to like and be liked

After completing an activity together, Ashley said to his foster carer: 'I am doing good listening now. Do you like it when I listen to you?' She replied: 'Yes, I love it because then we can have so much fun.'

Referral concerns from school and home

- Has lashed out at adults resulting in exclusion from school.
- Defiant; refusal to comply, only doing things on his terms, for example, wanting to sit where he chooses, refusing to join others at carpet time, wanting to be at the front of the line every time.
- Always seeking to take control, for example, sitting in teacher's chair and refusing to move, telling other children what to do.
- Tells authority figures: 'You can't tell me what to do', 'I go deaf, I can't hear you.'
- Conflict with teacher and foster carer, adults feel undermined.
- Rejects help or guidance, resulting in frustration, refusal or tantrum.
- With peers, he will take things, has difficulty sharing equipment, always wants to be first or chosen to answer, behaves as if he is unaware of his peers' feelings.
- Difficulty at transition times: changing lessons, going in and out to play, going from home to school. He wants to finish what he is doing with no regard for school expectations.
- He has a constant need to know when or what next, even if he does not want to participate. At home, as soon as a future event is mentioned he persists in asking repeatedly for all the details.
- He constantly refers to food, for example, asking when the next meal will be, 'What is for tea?' or repeatedly says 'I'm hungry'.
- His demeanour is that of a much younger child, toddlerish in his impulsivity; his tantrums show a lack of understanding of others' feelings.

Ashley's strengths as seen by the team

- He has a good memory.
- He enjoys music and singing.
- He responds well to outdoor activities.
- He is interested in nature.

- He is energetic.
- He can be gentle and thoughtful.
- He is honest, owns up, never tries to blame others.

Understanding and making sense of the concerns raised

This referral showed many typical features of a vulnerable child with attachment difficulties. The behaviour was that which would be expected of a child who had suffered difficulties in their earliest experiences. When a child is unsure of how or if a parent is going to respond to them, they suffer not only a lack of consistent reassuring warmth and responsiveness to their needs but also lose trust that others can meet their needs. Ashley's behaviour indicated that he was used to finding his own solutions and was hyper-alert both to opportunities to get what he wanted and to anything that might thwart him. This resulted in him developing very controlling behaviour and an inability to acknowledge the role of a responsible adult. Survival had been a driving force for him and entry to school faced him with experiences that were confusing and seemingly made threatening demands. Ashley regarded the adults as being 'unkind' when they needed to organise what he was to do and establish normal school routines that he was expected to accept without question.

Anxiety levels are rapidly raised in a child such as Ashley, for whom previously potentially frightening experiences were not soothed, for example, being alone, loud noises, discomfort through cold, hunger or pain, people shouting or being hurt. For Ashley, it seemed likely that the unexpected triggered the same feeling of anxiety in him that he had been aware of from early in his life. These highly-anxious feelings resulted in 'flight or fight' responses of running out of the classroom, and at these times he would lash out if an adult came too near.

Triggers such as loud noises, too many people, someone approaching from behind, sight of an unknown adult, instantaneously created internal panic, causing him to react in what were perceived as seemingly extreme and unpredictable ways.

For Ashley, transition times awoke his insecurities and anxiety about 'What next?' and again, he was frequently triggered into fight or flight mode. He would either take off, leaving the group to find some reassurance in a task of his own choosing, or he would refuse to leave where he was to join the group when it moved to another area or activity. This was a pattern at his new school, where he would refuse to leave the playground, he would run out of class when a new lesson was being prepared and would refuse to leave the classroom to go to the hall.

Ashley's perceived needs and individual targets

For Ashley, the priorities to address were decided to tackle were:

- To overcome and manage anxieties about transition.
- To establish trust so that he could feel safe enough to relinquish his need to be controlling of others.
- To develop an understanding of how others feel so he could understand the need to take turns, share, show kindness.
- To soothe and give him the experience of his vulnerability being contained.

Strategies used by the team to support Ashley's needs

Establishing trust

Early in Ashley's introduction to the group, everyone said aloud or sang the following group beliefs:

> We are kind to each other.
> We follow instructions.
> We keep ourselves and each other safe.
> We look after the Wellie Wednesday environment.

Throughout the day these ideals were then identified in words and actions and praise was given to reinforce that they had been noticed and were important, for example: 'That was kind of you to let someone else go first', 'Well done for keeping us safe by picking that up, someone could have tripped on it.' By making explicit references to kindness and safety, Ashley was able to feel reassured, thereby reducing his anxiety. As well as receiving praise himself he was also exposed to hearing those surrounding him being identified as kind, thoughtful, helpful, generous, a further reassurance of the safety of the group.

Ashley also needed to learn that it was safe for him to relinquish his need to be in control because adults can be trustworthy. He was provided with many opportunities to experience the adults as reliable. When a request from him, 'Can I go to the woods?' was responded to with, 'Not yet, but later you can', then he would be reminded: 'Ashley, you remember you wanted to go to the woods and we said later, well now we can go.'

A day plan was used so that children could see that the adults had planned what was going to happen. Ashley was able to learn that the team was in control of the day, what they said was true and they remembered what he said, so he experienced consistency and reliability and was able to begin to build trust.

Providing reassurance through structure

The day plan was a visual reassurance to the children for whom the unknown is scary. It consisted of a laminated A3 sheet on which were printed pictures to represent the structure of the day: breakfast, snack, lunch, compliments circle, final farewell. In addition, each of the day's activities was represented and stuck onto the chart at the start of the day. At any time, the children could be reminded to look on the chart if they needed to. For Ashley, it was important that he could see all the mealtimes were a permanent fixed part of the chart. Every time he wailed 'I'm hungry' he was reassured: 'That's OK to feel hungry because look on the chart and you will see that we are going to have snack/lunch.'

For Ashley, specific issues were aroused by food, its importance and availability. To demonstrate explicitly the laminated day plan had snack and mealtimes incorporated whilst the other activities were removable as they changed from week to week.

In later weeks, an indicator of the progress he was making became evident as he was able to enjoy the playful excitement and anticipation built up around the cook's special 'Wait and See Dessert'. Ashley was by now secure in the knowledge there would be a dessert, so he was able to cope with the uncertainty of not knowing exactly what it would be.

Initially, the day plan was carried with us to each activity so there was never a time when his need to know could not be responded to immediately and reassuringly. Soon, he was able to study the chart independently and his references to hunger and food ceased, as did his need for the chart to be with us at all times; he was happy to set it up at breakfast, then hang it on a hook by the fire where everyone knew where it was.

Clarifying expectations

The target chart was introduced as a reminder of the group expectations, for example, good sitting, good waiting, good thinking, good helping, etc. Each time a group member was caught getting it right they were specifically praised: 'Well done, that was good waiting for your turn.' Periodically during the day, the chart was referred to and individuals remembered what they or others had got right and ticks were added to each target. Ticks were added to the group target chart so there was a cooperative rather than competitive element to adding ticks to the shared chart.

In this way, the expectations were reinforced and the children became familiar with the vocabulary of the targets and learnt to enjoy receiving praise. Hand signs, sayings, songs and visual aids to eliminate the need for negotiation, disagreement or reprimands, Ashley's previously expected forms of communication.

Building empathy

When questions were used to seek repetitive answers, as was a common feature of Ashley's behaviour at home and school, the notion that perhaps he already knew the answer was introduced. When a repeated question was asked the response was: 'Read my mind, what am I going to say?' This taught Ashley that he could rely on consistent responses from the adults, for example, he would always need boots on to go in the woods; learning to anticipate what others might be thinking is an important stepping stone to building empathy. What might have become a battle, 'Do I have to put my boots on?', was defused by a new thinking challenge: 'Read my mind Ashley, what am I going to say?' He laughed and put his boots on. 'Wow Ashley, you do know what I was thinking!'

Another way of extending his understanding of empathy was with the phrase, 'Great minds think alike.' Ashley (and others) would get very upset if another child was asked for an idea or answer, and came up with the same as he had been going to say. Ashley would sulk and pout: 'He stole my answer.' It was explained to him that sometimes people do think the same thing, especially when it is a right answer, and that instead of minding he could give them a thumbs up and say, 'Great minds think alike.' This gave Ashley a positive way of expressing that he had had the answer too and was another way of building cooperation rather than competition.

Hearing others talking of how they felt, when dealing with comfortable and uncomfortable feelings, helped him to realise that other people have feelings that may be the same or different from his, for example, for some children going into the woods took courage to overcome their fearfulness, whilst for Ashley it held great excitement. Assuming there is only one way to feel results in 'I'm right and you are wrong' attitudes. By labelling feelings as they arose and acknowledging them, the children were able to learn that they could encourage each other and be sympathetic, instead of resorting to the previously used put-downs or dismissive comments when someone felt differently to them.

> It is not always obvious to children, especially whilst at an egocentric stage of their development, that everyone else does not feel the same as them. This needs to be made explicit so that being able to work out how someone else might be feeling becomes a possibility. Developing empathy also requires learning how to make sympathetic and compassionate responses. Some of the most challenging children are those who do not lack empathy, they can read others' feelings but without compassion. They then gain control from using their knowledge to create irritation, distress or fear.

Taking turns following and leading

In order for Ashley to relinquish his need for control we needed to offer him opportunities when we would follow his lead, so in turn he could follow ours. Music proved a perfect vehicle for this exchange. Instruments were set out and Ashley was quick to choose the biggest drum. He banged with all his might and huge enjoyment. When a music specialist (Pitt, J.)[1] started to play her tambourine copying his rhythms, a moment of intense connection quickly developed. He looked up from the drum and held her gaze as he realised she was exactly mimicking his every drum beat. When he looked away she changed the rhythm and he followed and again held her gaze with a look of delight. There followed a few more minutes of swapping as they played 'follow my leader' with the instruments. This brief, and to the onlooker, almost imperceptible, exchange marked another significant deepening of his understanding; Ashley had in that brief moment of cooperation experienced the joy of following as well as leading. He and his foster carer then repeated the game and when the instruments were put away he returned to sit contentedly cuddled up against her. Earliest attachment bonding and attunement stem from the baby and mother's gaze interactions (Gerhardt 2004). As Ashley experienced having his gaze held it seemed that contentment followed as he movingly and affectionately sought out his foster carer.

Limited choice

'I'll do it when you stop telling me to' was one of Ashley's sayings, showing how hard it was for him to feel that following instructions was a safe and beneficial thing to do. Ashley preferred to make his own decisions but when given two choices he would usually be able to decide on one or other. His cognitive developmental stage was typical of a much younger child for whom this approach is better suited. So Ashley was distracted from defiance by the thinking required to make a choice. On one occasion he had failed to join the group. He then tried to distract everyone by throwing leaves. He was taken aside to remove the audience and offered two good choices, to go and sit in the circle or go to sit with an adult away from the group. The change of emphasis then enabled him to respond positively to what had previously caused him to dig his heels in.

Impact on the family

As Ashley learnt that compliance was not a punishment, and even brought benefits, he was able to identify what was helpful. He was overheard saying to his foster carer, 'I am doing good listening now. Do you like it when I listen to you?' She responded, 'Yes I love it because then we can have so much fun', followed by a big hug.

Ashley's love of physical activity and the observations showing how much longer he could sustain an activity and concentrate when there was a physical 'doing' element to it led to keeping a daily outdoor element to his home routine. Seeing Ashley enjoying himself outside gave his foster carer pleasure; she bought him a cart and a small trampoline and gave him a digging area in the garden. Digging as large a hole as possible is a very satisfying activity for children, no further purpose is required than the rewarding experience of seeing it grow as a result of their own physical effort. Going back over time to continue the excavation helps to illustrate how persistence over time brings results. Watching a pile of earth grow can serve as additional visual evidence of the effort made and provides a secondary activity of carting it away to another area.

His foster carer saw the benefits of ignoring the negative comments and behaviour whilst increasing the amount of praise she could give. Adopting the positive targets of looking for the good and giving praise helped her to keep the focus on the positives Ashley was mastering. Realising other children also had difficulties made her feel less isolated as she tried to compensate for Ashley's difficult start in life. Being part of a group gave her the chance to see Ashley interacting in gentle and thoughtful ways. When coming for lunch in Week three and hearing another child objecting to the decision that the adults were to be served first, he said: 'I think the grown-ups should be served first, they deserve it.' This was a particularly significant sign that he was feeling safe and content given his previous preoccupation with worrying if there would be enough food.

Changes noticed in Ashley

For Ashley, a significant development in his understanding of the link between the targets, getting it right and positive feelings, was when we took the group to meet Megan the sheepdog. Everything her owner, Kevin, said was acted upon and to the children's amazement, as she worked with the sheep they saw her doing all their getting it right targets, except good speaking! Kevin told the children how Megan had had an unhappy home where she had not been understood and seemed to be no good, but he took her in and by being kind and patient with her she had become a brilliant sheepdog. Ashley watched as she did:

- Good looking.
- Good listening.

- Good following instructions.
- Good cooperation.
- Good concentrating.
- Good thinking.
- Good sitting.
- Good waiting.
- Good ignoring.

She ignored everything except what Kevin was telling her to do, even when the children were told by Kevin to try to call her. Ashley also noticed how happy she looked with her tail wagging and she was so eager to get on with her work. 'She really loves Kevin doesn't she?' he observed, so had internalised that cooperating, helping and being helped were more than just work as they also built the bonds of affection. He moved closer to his foster carer and slipped his hand into hers as they walked back.

Transferring learning into school

Transition times increase anxiety in vulnerable children because they inevitably highlight their sense of dread around the question 'what next?' and for them it is associated with fear of the unknown. If adults can be aware of this and instil a sense of control, for example, 'I am going to tell you what we will be doing next' or 'I have planned that next we will be doing …', then calm is more easily maintained.

Visual timetable

In order to reduce anxiety, a visual timetable can be reassuring as it maps out the day and is best combined with a support assistant giving a brief outline of the content of the next lesson. For some children, the content of lessons can prove to be emotive for them, for example, the language in maths – take away, split, remove – may all have a difficult connotation for looked-after children (LAC). Supportive adults who can forewarn and deal sensitively with issues that arise can mean that the child's 'unthinkable' thoughts become, with help, manageable. Use of the concepts of comfortable and uncomfortable feelings (PATHS) are helpful at these times: 'I can see you are having difficulty with some uncomfortable feelings at the moment. Take time to do some calming breathing until you feel better.'

Take-up time

It was suggested to Ashley's foster carers and teacher that he needed 'take-up time' before being expected to act on an instruction. In addition, five-minute warnings of an imminent change, were given; for example, finishing play before bed or ending a piece of work. When an activity was concluding an adult would speak directly to Ashley saying, 'Ashley, it will be time to finish this in five minutes, then we will be going to …' No further conversation was entered into to give him time to process the information. After five minutes he was helped to finish with limited choice decisions, for example, 'We need to put this away now, will you clear up the … or the …' As he cleared up he was given a responsibility towards the next task, for example, 'I will need you to carry my clip board for me.' In these ways, transition times were supported and the distractions of choice or responsibility helped keep his feelings of anxiety at bay. In school, his teacher found she could prevent a confrontation in the playground by sending him into the classroom ahead to put her register ready on her chair with her pen.

At times, particularly when a change of activity or moving to a different place were imminent, Ashley would become oppositional and defiant, and this would also bring a spate of swearing and abusive language. His teacher found that reminding herself these were words he had heard and probably had directed at him, helped her to see she did not need to take them personally. She also took time to explain to Ashley that: 'These are words I know too but we don't use them in school. You don't hear the adults in school using these words, so you don't need to use them either.'

In some cases where young children are using inappropriate language, staff need to be prepared to talk about the words that are OK in school and the ones that are not OK. How is a child supposed to know which words are regarded as swear words in school if they hear them frequently used outside of school? Ashley learnt through kindly instruction what was and was not acceptable.

> Sometimes, words regarded as inappropriate in school have even been heard as terms of endearment. When one teenage student had been accused of swearing by a peer, she turned for support from a teacher saying: 'Little b****, that's not swearing is it Miss?' Before reaching it is often enlightening to know what a child thinks the meaning is of an unacceptable word they are using. Such investigating is unemotive and serves to deflate the value of a word that had seemed to the child to be empowering.

Feeling safe

When Ashley left the group at his safety was addressed by reminding him: 'We need to keep you safe so you must stay with the group.' Similarly, his class teacher transferred this into school by reminding him: 'It is my job as a grown-up to make sure you are safe so I need to know where you are, if you leave the classroom I won't know where you have gone.' These reminders are a way of reassuring a vulnerable child that they are liked and people care for them. The brain responds to its innate survival need for safety and social connection (Porges 2007). For Ashley, use of the words *safe*, *care*, *trust* and *kind* proved transformational. His teacher noticed how much more responsive he was to following an instruction using these positive words. She also found him accepting her role of responsible adult with fewer challenges to her authority once she used: 'I am the grown-up here and it is my job to look after you.' When Ashley wanted to take control she would say: 'That is not a job/decision/ choice for children, you can trust me as a grown-up to do that.' On arrival in her class, he had as often as possible moved to sit in her chair. Rather than leaving him in order not to avoid a confrontation, she used it as an opportunity to remind him that he did not need to try to be the adult because she was there. Given this emphasis, Ashley conceded the place and began his successful transition to understanding how school works. Ashley was starting to develop a new understanding of the differing roles of a child and a responsible adult. With less need to control and reduced anxiety, a more relaxed Ashley began to enjoy appropriate play, conversation, laughter and fun.

Key strategies used

- Building trust through shared beliefs.
- Reassurance through structure.
- Clarification of expectation.
- Building empathy: 'read my mind' and 'great minds think alike'.
- Turn-taking, following and leading.
- Limited choice.
- Managing transition: take-up time, visual timetable, keeping safe.

Reflection

If anger is a secondary emotion, what might be the primary drive in a child who exhibits anger? How can a school behaviour policy incorporate appropriate responses to anxiety-driven challenging behaviour?

Note

1 Pitt, J. Tutor, MA early years music at Centre for Research in Early Childhood; Visiting lecturer, University of Roehampton.

References

Gerhardt, S. (2004). *Why love matters: How affection shapes a baby's brain*. London: Brunner-Routledge.
Greenberg, M. Kusche, C. (1995). *Promoting Alternative Thinking Strategies (PATHS)* Pub. U.S. Channing-Bete Company.
Porges, S.W. (2007). The poly vagal theory: Neurophysical foundations of emotions, attachment communications and self regulation. New York: W.W. Norton and Company.

Chapter 6

Sammy

Finding the need to speak

> Wellie Wednesday is really fun and then my work is good.
>
> (Sammy)

Referral concerns from school and home

- Sammy makes noises and uses a whining voice instead of speaking.
- He fails to participate by:
  - not answering questions
  - not completing work.
- He lacks engagement with peers. He opts out by:
  - wandering off
  - rolling on the floor
  - becoming absorbed in playing or handling objects.
- He fails to speak in sentences.
- He lacks physical coordination.
- He is unsafe in the playground because he does not reliably return and fails to respond to safety warnings.
- The Educational Psychologist considered the need for a diagnosis of Autistic Spectrum Disorder and a special school placement.

Sammy's strengths as seen by the team

- He has a fascination for living creatures and the world around him.
- He has a close relationship with his father.
- He shows independence and a desire to explore.
- He is able to read well, especially non-fiction information.
- He invents his own amusement.
- He has physical stamina; he and his father walked a long distance to and from school each day.
- He is exuberant and loves to run and whirl about, he enjoys chasing and being chased.

Understanding and making sense of the concerns raised

The school showed concern over Sammy's difficulty with the normal boundaries and expectations for classroom and playground behaviour. It was apparent that the team would need to draw Sammy into the group and help him to realise that he could make a positive contribution. It was also important to help Sammy realise that he would benefit by being part of the group.

Sammy's father told us that he had seen a paediatrician, who had told him that Sammy suffered from 'demand avoidance syndrome' and that the Educational Psychologist was considering his suitability for a special school placement.

We were concerned that given his strengths, perhaps his avoidant behaviour could be driven by a different cause. For example, could his failure to participate be caused by a lack of understanding of expectations or inadequate language comprehension? It was important to check whether his difficulties were rooted in a lack of expectation, rather than understanding. Was his poor verbal communication a speech and language issue, or due to poor social skills? It was evident that there was a need to establish our expectations about speaking clearly and to help him to understand that by speaking audibly and clearly his wishes would be more likely to be met. With these questions in mind, we considered what targets would be the most appropriate for him.

Sammy' s perceived needs and individual targets

- Developing a positive self-image.
- To use words to express himself instead of using a whining voice or pointing.
- To stay with the group and join in with the group activities.
- To answer when a question is directed at him, for example, 'Would you like a drink of water?'
- To understand that a group instruction, for example, 'We are all going to the woods now' includes him, even though his name has not been said.
- To focus and to listen with attention.

Strategies used by the team to support Sammy's needs

Change the language to change the behaviour

We realised that clear communication was needed from the adults and Sammy. Adults did not interpret Sammy's noises or gesturing, however obvious his meaning was, but kindly and calmly used phrases such as:

> 'Sammy I don't know what those sounds mean. You need to say it in words', 'Speak with your mouth not with your hands' (when he was pointing, touching or gesturing), 'We need to know what you are thinking/feeling so tell us in words.'

On his first day, Sammy made a strange high-pitched whining noise as he pointed, indicating that he wanted cereal. Our response was, 'Would you like Cheerios, Weetabix or muesli?' This ensured that Sammy had been given the required words to use but when he continued to whine the next child was asked and served whilst Sammy was told in a calm and matter of fact voice: 'I'll come back to you when you stop making that noise Sammy.' Sammy listened as the next two children chose and poured their cereal and milk. When it was his turn again he was told: 'I'm sorry I couldn't understand what you meant Sammy, when you made noises, so I need you to say in words what you would like. Would you like Cheerios, Weetabix or muesli?' This time Sammy answered loud and clear and triumphantly took his bowl of Cheerios to a seat by the fire. He ate and listened, and shortly after this when our role model puppet was introduced, it was Sammy who suggested a name for the puppet in a clear voice. His father beamed and realised that he must expect Sammy to speak clearly in order to express himself. Sammy's difficulty may not have been due to a lack of comprehension but was possibly due to low expectations. Adults had followed his gestures and guessed what he wanted. Though meant kindly, this had reduced his need to speak. In this new situation, Sammy began to realise that if he used precise and accurate speech, others would understand him, and his needs would be more successfully met.

The adults modelled an expectation of clear and accurate communication by:

- Querying a meaning or offering an accurate version to be repeated, instead of responding to the gist of what was being said.
- Always encouraging extending responses from key words to full sentences, for example, at breakfast 'Cheerios' was replaced by 'I'd like Cheerios please'.

Unless a child repeats a whole sentence, extended language does not readily embed in their thinking. In order to progress, they need to be able to memorise longer word chains and hear themselves saying them. It requires a higher cognitive function to specify meaning accurately, for example, 'Cheerios' could have a multitude of meanings other than wanting to eat them now! Without understanding the need for precision and accuracy in speech, a child will also be hampered in the necessary progression required for developing good problem-solving and reasoning skills.

Using limited choice to avoid opposition

Use of limited choice allows the child to maintain some control whilst following an instruction. The adults always offered children specific choices that included the required vocabulary. A choice was specified so that the child could respond using the vocabulary they had just heard, for example: 'Choose which to put on first, your boots or your coat' or 'You need to sit down to listen now; choose the bench or the chair.'

Sammy was used to doing his own thing, joining in or not, according to his mood. When he wandered away from the group on the first day, his father moved anxiously towards him to try to cajole him into returning. It was suggested to his father that he choose a chair himself (i.e model the correct behaviour). Then a member of staff, without telling Sammy what he was doing wrong, said 'Sammy you need to come to the fire now. You can choose to sit on the bench with the children or the chair next to your dad … (pause) … Hurry, we don't want you to miss finding out what we are going to do next.' This was followed by a longer pause so Sammy could process the information, then 'So, bench or chair, decide quickly or I will have to decide for you.' At this point, Sammy started heading back to the fire so all that was needed was: 'Well done Sammy, you made a good choice.'

Giving clear instructions and listening with attention

Adults were careful to be clear in giving instructions and exact explanations were given to clarify   expectations. For some children, trying to interpret what 'pay attention' or 'listen' really means can be confusing. We noticed that Sammy was always listening and that even at a distance he was taking in information, so for him, wandering around the classroom did not mean he was not listening. To help him understand, we prefaced 'good listening' with explicit instructions for how others would know when he was listening:

> 'We need you to show us you are doing good listening and to help others by not distracting them. You need to have:

> - A still body.
> - Eyes concentrating.
> - Ears ready to hear instructions/explanation/what happens in the story.
> - Lips closed, "remember it is the ears' turn to listen and the mouth's turn to do good waiting".'

Praise was given as soon possible: 'Well done, that is good sitting, I can see you are ready to do good listening.'

When adults repeated an instruction they used exactly the same words so a change of vocabulary would not confuse a child. This allowed a child, who was failing to process the information fast and accurately enough, the chance to catch up as they heard the identical instruction repeated.

If, after this and extra 'take-up time', an instruction was not being followed, then a check for comprehension was made using a calm friendly tone, i.e. the expectation is that non-compliance is due to a lack of comprehension rather than disobedience. Such a reminder might be: 'What is it you need to do now?' This then either elicits the correct response or allows the instruction to be repeated if the answer was 'I don't know'.

Eavesdropping and the use of compliments

Talking about a child positively within their hearing is a powerful way for a child to hear good things about themselves. Some children find accepting praise difficult. Overhearing two adults talking about what they can do or achieve seems less deniable.

If a child in difficulty can overhear ('eavesdrop' on) another child getting it right, it can help them to absorb what it is they need to be doing. For example, another child was wanting to tread on insects to kill them. Instead of giving him attention by trying to stop him, Sammy was nearby, and was immediately praised for his kindness: 'Sammy you are so kind putting the worm back under its log. Well done for remembering we are the visitors here but it is the woodland creatures' home.'

This action was referred to at circle time in Sammy's compliment of the day, which reinforced his kindness. This had a two-fold effect. Firstly, Sammy heard a compliment about himself so he could begin to reconstruct his self-image: 'I am kind and I have a good memory'. Secondly, the other child received no reinforcement (attention) for his planned action, but heard positive reinforcement being given to Sammy, helping him to internalise that praise was gained for being kind.

Developing a positive sense of self

Sammy had been somewhat isolated at school. He did not become engaged in group activities and he rarely remained in assembly until the end. It was important to ensure that Sammy could experience himself differently, as a participator in the group and a contributor of ideas.

An internal self-image is built up based on external and internal influences. When a child hears himself talked about as difficult, naughty, shy, different, strange, angry, these are the characteristics the child will associate with himself. When his internal dialogue reinforces this image with statements such as 'I can't', 'I'm rubbish' and 'No-one likes me', this self-image becomes entrenched.

Our aim was to reconstruct Sammy's image of himself by noticing all the good things and reframing the negatives in a more favourable light. Through receiving praise for his interest and concern for the wildlife, Sammy recognised his strength and was keen to learn more; gradually he ceased to withdraw from the group. As he experienced the enjoyment of being a part of the group, he started wanting to make sure he did not miss out by leaving the group.

Feeling part of a group, making a positive contribution

The team aimed to ensure that Sammy felt part of the group and enjoyed the positive experiences that resulted from this. As we gathered around the campfire for the first time, Sammy's attention was held only momentarily by the excitement of the fire. After a short while he wandered away. This was an opportunity for Sammy to experience his behaviour being ignored rather than being chased and brought back. Instead, the message was given that he was part of the group and that missing out would be sad for him: 'Oh dear, you might have missed what the group was doing we'd like you to stay with us.'

Feeling needed and experiencing a sense of belonging are vital human affiliative attributes, but for children exhibiting challenging behaviour, school frequently becomes a place where these feelings are experienced less and less. Often, in school the opposite may occur, for example, being sent out of a class. This can result in feelings of rejection and isolation. Whilst useful deterrents for most children, for those who have experienced real rejection or isolation, they are likely to produce high levels of anxious arousal that are not conducive to compliant acceptance of sanctions, hence some children's violent outbursts when withdrawal is attempted.

Within the group, the aim was for everyone to experience a warm sense of belonging, so every opportunity was taken to express this. Comments were used that sent the message that each child was liked and needed in the group. When made to feel special by a personal inclusive comment, the pleasurable feelings experienced will be sufficient for the person to want to experience more of that feel-good factor. When children expressed negative attitudes towards themselves, wanting to exclude themselves from joining in or being part of the group, they would be asked, 'Would it be the same without you?' or told, 'We'd miss you'. No response was required, but the message of acceptance had been heard. Sometimes negative responses were elicited but these were not engaged with in order not to feed the negativity.

Impact on the family

It was quickly apparent that Sammy and his father had a close relationship. Sammy would seek physical reassurance from his father and they worked well together. His father enjoyed being outdoors, saying it reminded him of his childhood visits to his grandparents in the country. Initially, he was on edge, anticipating difficulties, as Sammy's school experience had always been problematic. Together they entered into the whole experience, delighting in new successes, especially in Sammy's conversations, his participation in discussions and sharing ideas. Sammy's father said that Sammy had created his own Wellie Wednesday area at the bottom of his garden where he liked to go and play.

Two years later an independent researcher (Belton 2014) asked Sammy's father about his experience of Wellie Wednesday. In an extract from that interview he said:

It was nice to see Sammy getting involved with other children. Before, everything had to be laid on for him, it was nice to see him going out in the woods and doing things, he started thinking for himself ... before, I had to keep him indoors, I couldn't let him out. I think it opened up a new world for him. It's shown up at school, he used to misbehave and get sent home. Now you can't keep him out of school, he wants to go. At Wellie Wednesday he had to tow the line to get where he wanted to be and that did help a lot ... It's changed the way I do things now I know you have to be firm and tell him what you expect.

All the children changed ... started to notice things, got inventive and 'final circle time' helped when you thought about the people around you and each individual. It certainly worked well for Sammy and I could see it worked for the other children as well. It worked for the adults as well; a lot of us were pretty on our own with our children and so it was good to meet up with others.

His step-mum added: 'He's done brilliant, he's more independent now, doesn't need one-to-one help anymore.'

Changes noticed in Sammy

Sammy began to stay within the group. He made a positive contribution, volunteering ideas and communicating clearly. He showed a great interest in the environment, looking closely at fungi that were growing and caring about small creatures. He loved jumping in the leaves and collecting things of interest. Sammy made good progress in every way; he listened, thought, contributed ideas, was kind and cooperative to others, made us laugh with his sense of humour and showed enthusiasm for each day's new opportunities.

On the last day he showed how far he had come from the little boy who had initially seemed so isolated. It was a glorious autumn day and the fallen leaves in the woods excited the children. It was Sammy who said: 'Come on, let's see how big a pile we can make to jump in.' He then galvanised the others into action collecting brooms and choosing a space for their leaf pile. All worked happily and eagerly together, culminating in taking it in turns to jump into their impressive pile of leaves.

Two years later when Sammy was asked what he especially liked about Wellie Wednesday, he replied without hesitation: 'My idea on the last day to make a pile of leaves and jump in it.' Such simple experiences held within them profound moments of significant change for the children. In this case, Sammy had learnt that he could engage and organise others to participate in his idea. This was possible because he had grasped that he needed to communicate his ideas verbally and interact positively with others. In this way, Wellie Wednesday's activities contained within them transferable skills that Sammy was able to take back into his school and home environments.

Transferring learning into school

Sammy changed schools and settled well into his new school where it was decided, because he was doing well, that he did not need the Nurture Group that was on offer. The staff in school soon said he was no longer requiring one-to-one support. His learning was progressing and he was able to socialise with his peer group. He particularly enjoyed running and playground chasing games.

A team member visited him in school and he spoke clearly and happily about Wellie Wednesday and what he remembered: the leaves, the mushrooms, the bubbles and trying to fly kites. He drew a picture of himself and the visiting team member at Wellie Wednesday. He drew a tree with a branch, a nest and a red squirrel (they were bred at the Countryside Centre). He wrote a speech bubble that said: 'It's nice to see you again.'

Key strategies used

- Changing the language to change the behaviour.
- Using limited choice to avoid opposition.
- Giving clear instructions.
- Encouraging listening with attention.
- 'Eavesdropping', hearing good things said about himself.
- Giving and receiving compliments.
- Developing a positive sense of self.
- Feeling part of a group, making a positive contribution.

Reflection

When children do not communicate clearly, could failure to participate be caused by a lack of expectation rather than a lack of understanding? Do children understand what 'listen' and 'pay attention' mean?

Reference

Belton, T. (2014). *Happier people healthier planet: How putting wellbeing first would help sustain life on Earth*. Bristol: Silver Wood Books.

Chapter 7

Ella

Attention seeking or attention needing?

The best bit of my life is being at home. Sometimes me and Mummy used to fall out but now I am keeping on the right lines and me and Mummy are friends, I like it. That is 'check and change' isn't it?

(Ella)

Referral concerns from school and home

- Ella disrupts the classroom with her frequent interruptions calling out or causing a disturbance.
- At home her incessant talk exhausts and frustrates her adoptive parents.
- She asks constant repetitive questions.
- She has difficulties maintaining friendships because of her controlling ways.
- Her safety is at risk from obsessive chewing and eating of non-food items, for example, pencils, paper, plastic.
- At home her relationship with food is a source of exasperation.
- She has a desperate need to avoid silence. She interrupts, rather than remain out of the class teacher's attention by quietly getting on with her work.
- She has an overriding need to know 'what next?' which prevents her from engaging with being in the present.
- It seems as if she holds the belief that because she wants something to happen it can, and tearful distress follows when things don't work out as she wanted them to.

Ella's strengths as seen by the team

- Her enthusiasm and willingness to participate in activities.
- She has a great love of music and singing.
- She has a remarkable ability to memorise words, sayings and songs with ease.
- She has a wonderfully creative imagination.

Understanding and making sense of concerns raised

Ella's referral concerns all spoke of a child with an attachment-based difficulty. Her early life with whatever traumas she had lived through had resulted in behaviour that ensured she could not be forgotten. Her extreme need for biting and chewing and constant references to food suggested that she had lived with the experience, and subsequent fear, of being hungry. When Ella became obsessed with an idea, she exhibited the thinking and behaviour of a younger child still in the developmental phase of 'magical thinking'. This was evident when Ella was watching the sheepdog at work: once she saw lambs her only thought was of wanting to hold one. She was unable to accept that this was not going to happen because the lambs would not like it. From then on she could no longer enjoy the moment of seeing the dog work nor understand that she was spoiling the experience with her outcries. Ella's struggles with her peers were clearly due to her inability to understand others, indicating her developmental stage of egocentricity.

Magical thinking and egocentricity

This is when a child believes that 'wishes come true'. It is a normal developmental stage that coincides with when children are also egocentric in their outlook. Sometimes it persists, in extreme cases children may have wished for things to happen that then occurred, thus entrenching their belief and prolonging the stage. If something unfortunate happens during the phase of magical thinking, e.g. a parent leaves home or a child is placed in care, then the child may carry guilt and be left feeling responsible.

Ella's perceived needs and individual targets

- Ella needed help to understand other people's needs and views so as to develop empathy.
- Ella needed to experience quiet times positively. She needed to be able to feel safe and calm when no-one was talking.
- She needed to be able to trust staff enough to relinquish her need to constantly need to know 'what next'.

Strategies used by the team to support Ella's needs

Building trust

When Ella asked repetitive questions, most frequently about 'what next?' a hand sign of three fingers was used to remind her of the words 'wait and see', a saying used and then taught to the group as a song (© J. Pitt, sung to the tune of 'Frère Jacques').

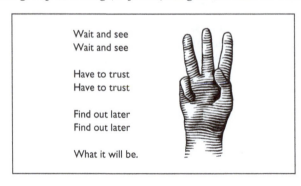

Wait and see
Wait and see

Have to trust
Have to trust

Find out later
Find out later

What it will be.

The concept of trust was introduced because for children who have experienced unreliable adults in their early lives it is not surprising that they learn to rely on themselves and try to keep control. In order to establish trust, it was vitally important for us to keep our word to Ella. This was demonstrated by returning to each unanswered question at the right time and pointing out that we had not forgotten her question and her need to know. Gradually Ella was able to understand that not only did we remember and keep our word but also we showed her that through our Day Plan she could *trust us* to know what we were going to do throughout the day.

Gradually, experience taught her that all would be well with the unfolding of the day and soon she was increasingly able to feel the enjoyment of anticipation. 'Wait and See' became a mantra for good surprises and enjoyable experiences, where previously, any element of surprise induced anxiety or fear.

The use of non-verbal communication

Ella's use of a visual Day Plan and the 'wait and see' sign were initial ways of using non-verbal communication to help clarify expectations and demonstrate our control over the day. To overcome Ella's intrusive and demanding verbal contributions we continued to extend the use of hand signs, sayings, songs and visual aids. We were fortunate to have a music specialist volunteer, who converted our many sayings and beliefs into songs to add to our Wellie Wednesday song book, written by a member of the team. Ella took to singing these with delight, having a very musical ear, she loved to sing and learnt the words with ease. By using one of her strengths and pleasures, we were able to reinforce the messages that would help her manage what was difficult for her.

> Just a minute, let me think
> Let me think, let me think
>
> Just a minute, let me think
> Think before I do.
>
> Just a minute, let me think
> Let me think, let me think
> Just a minute, let me think
> Think before I say.
>
> (Sung to the tune of "London Bridge is falling down")

Using puppets and stories devised to address her needs also worked very well. Ella was excited and affectionate towards the various characters introduced. These included:

- Crunch the Croc who had a problem knowing what he should and should not eat.
- Stella, a puppet with a huge mouth who had difficulty stopping words from pouring out.
- Patience, a tortoise who knew how to do good waiting when it was not her turn to speak and who knew the benefits of not rushing at things, but taught that slowly and carefully works out better in the end.

Ella was delighted to tell us her good news:

> I used to get a good idea and have to say it. Now I know good waiting. I can keep it in until the other person stops the conversation.

The use of metaphor

The stories and characters were introduced to the group with no specific reference to any particular problem being identified as that of someone in the group. Stories, characters and puppets were used to engage the children's imagination at an emotional level, where the message could be more deeply assimilated. No explicit discussion of the meaning was entered into, since that would return to a cognitive level where the content may remain as just another story and not be fully absorbed. By keeping discussions at an imaginative 'play' level, the children were able to see its personal relevance and explore new ways of being.

The use of animal characters and their stories was also a way of allowing Ella to hear about the feelings of others. Ella's responses indicated she could understand their point of view. Her affectionate interaction with the animals indicated that she was developing and expressing sensitive, sympathetic and empathic qualities. From these safe explorations it was much easier for Ella to become aware of the feelings and needs of others.

Attention on positive behaviour

Ella's disruptive behaviour, such as interrupting during lessons, especially at listening and quiet times, was an attempt to gain attention. Keeping attention focused on the positive behaviour was therefore vital so that Ella did not need to resort to negative behaviour in order to attract adult attention.

Being ignored is the opposite of feeling part of a group. It is a powerful feeling connected to the potentially life-threatening fear of being forgotten. Children, for whom lack of attention has been a reality or risk in their early development, feel the need to gain attention at all costs in order to avoid the sense of fear and desperation associated with these early life experiences.

In addition, the children need to learn 'good ignoring' and be praised for it when one child is getting it wrong, otherwise focus will turn to the negative behaviour and others will join in. Immediate praise of the nearest child getting it right will usually act as a reminder of what is required to regain adult attention, for example, 'Well done for good listening', encourages the calling out child to quieten down because attention is gained by the listening behaviour.

Being kept in mind, not being forgotten

For children who have not developed secure attachments, fear of being forgotten is very real. When people disappear out of a child's life, or do not respond to their needs, then feeling safe is not a reality they have experienced. It is in knowing they are safely held in the mind of their closest adult(s) that children build resilience so that they can cope when they are not with them.

One way for children to experience how we hold them in mind when they were not with us was to make sure that at breakfast a reference was always made when a child was absent, for example, 'We will miss Freddie today.' Children would then know that if they were absent they too would not be forgotten. To make this even more explicit, the following week, instead of a compliment card, the previously absent child and their adult would receive a card to inform them that they had been missed.

We are sorry you were ill.

We missed you.

In addition, the children were given personalised compliments cards each week and photographs to be used as visible reminders of their successes. They were also reminded that as the cards and photographs were being prepared we were thinking about them, even though we weren't with them. One team member who was going to be absent the following week left a written message for the children to say she would be thinking of them even though she was unable to be there.

For those children who have had traumatic or chronically stressful early experiences, one of their greatest needs is to know that people are aware of them, i.e. they have not been forgotten. To achieve this they develop strategies that can prove demanding, often they are labelled as attention seeking but these behaviours can be symptomatic of 'attention needing'.

This need for attention conflicts with classroom expectations that there will be periods of quiet, group carpet listening sessions, assemblies and requirements to wait silently. For vulnerable children, deep-rooted anxieties can surface in any quiet space, and disruptive behaviour or verbal interruptions spring up to break the unbearable silence and its intrusive thoughts and disquieting feelings. The disruption usually ensures someone will turn their attention to and speak to them, albeit with displeasure.

To help Ella learn to resist making verbal interruptions we used a positively phrased alternative to 'no talking or don't talk'. She was taught that ears and mouth need to take turns and when it is the ears' turn to listen she needs to stop her mouth saying things. These concepts were introduced using a puppet called Stella, who had a huge mouth that kept getting her into trouble! As the puppet interacted with the wise old Turtle, Stella and Ella together learnt new strategies.

Listening to others

Ella needed help to understand that listening to others is important, interesting and could be helpful:

> A chinese proverb says:
> We have two ears and one mouth
> so ...
> We should listen
> Twice as much
> As we speak.

A wooden hare with large ears was used as a role model for the children. They were told about real hares who use their especially big ears that can move without needing to turn their head. They can hear sounds from all directions, therefore making them expert listeners. The photographs acted as a visual reminder and engagement with the hare's story and meant that the idea of good listening acquired positive associations; very different from feelings caused by thinking about not talking or not interrupting.

One child, three years later, spotted a team member in school and stopped for a chat, during which he said with a beaming smile: 'I still remember the hare and its ears.'

The concept of not doing something, for example, 'Don't talk', can only be interpreted by first registering the very thing that should not be happening i.e. talking. It is more successful to state the desired behaviour, in this case good listening. Pointing to or tapping the visual reminder photographs allowed for a non-verbal cue to be given in addition, if necessary.

> **Remember, it is your ears' turn to listen now whilst I read the story.**

The silent speech bubble

To further assist Ella, we gave her a large laminated empty speech bubble as a reminder that there were 'no words in it'. At first she needed to hold it, a tangible reminder of our expectation that she would keep words out of it whilst she was doing good listening. She also knew we would have to

return to her to collect it when listening time was over, a reinforcement that she could not therefore be forgotten. Soon we were able to keep the speech bubble visible and point to it if necessary. She was later able to use this as a transferable strategy for school. Other children, too, benefited from the visual reminder and class teachers found that by having a silent speech bubble on the wall they could silently point to it if a reminder was necessary. Ella told us: 'I think about the silent speech bubble helping me. When I used to call out it made everyone agitated and wasn't very nice. I thought there's no need.'

From another of her comments made on a follow-up visit, it seemed that she was using the speech bubble as a transitional object, i.e. revisiting the calm feeling she had during Wellie Wednesday.

> I've still got my silent speech bubble, it makes me feel relaxed. Before I came to Wellie Wednesday I used to be chatting and chatting but now when I feel like it and look at the silent speech bubble then I feel calm.

Soothing, reassuring strategies: transitional objects, time charts

Another strategy used during quiet times was to give something of ours to be held, for example, 'Please could you look after my pen whilst you are listening.' Children who worry they may be forgotten (whether consciously or subconsciously) are reassured by knowing the pen will have to be collected, so the adult cannot overlook them.

This idea was also used to help Ella cope with anxiety about transitions between term time and holidays. She was lent a toy from school to look after and knew she would need to return it at the beginning of the next term. This reassured her that she was going to return. During the project, cards and small reminder items linked to each week's activities were given to the children so they had tangible reminders of their positive experience.

> A transitional object, as defined by Winnicott (1971), is an item that serves a soothing function for children. A security object can give a child both emotional and tangible comfort, especially during times of stress.

The visual plan for the day proved reassuring to many of the children, so a chart was added that would visually show the children that they would be coming back the following week and for how many more sessions. The chart took the form of a piece of A4 paper divided into six squares. A butterfly picture was printed in each box and the page laminated. A second sheet was created with a caterpillar in each box. This too was laminated but then cut up. A caterpillar square was lightly attached over each butterfly. At final circle time each week a caterpillar was removed so it turned into a butterfly. The number of remaining caterpillars corresponded to the number of weeks left. The transition from caterpillar to butterfly also represented symbolically the theme of change.

When Ella became anxious and confused about how long the holidays would be, a similar chart was made in school for her to take home for the holiday, but this time using her own drawings. She was then able to keep track of how long it was until she returned to school. Its helpfulness and significance was fully realised when as the following holiday approached, Ella asked if she could make another butterfly chart.

Looked-after children who have been moved about within the care and education system may need reassurance that they will be returning to school. The butterfly chart showing how long until they return and an item or toy that can be borrowed and taken home for the holidays helps to ensure in the child's mind they will be coming back as they have to return the item. Evidence has shown (Geddes, 2006) that school can serve as a secure base. Teachers were always encouraged to remember that although children's behaviour can be challenging, schools can represent a place of safety. The continuity and support of a school with its familiar routines and caring adults can have an enormous effect on the resilience and success of a troubled child. The efforts to which some schools were prepared to go for individual pupils was heart-warming and exemplary.

Making friends with silent stillness

For some children, silence is anxiety-raising. These are children for whom as a baby their need for reassurance and comfort was not adequately met or was inconsistent, and as a consequence their greatest fear is of being forgotten. For these children, any attention is better than none, so they often appear unrepentant for the disturbances they cause.

Learning to relax and use the Rainbow Garden visualisation helped Ella to enjoy times of 'silent stillness', channelling her vivid imagination into pleasurable thoughts. The guided visualisation was combined with using calming 7/11 breathing, focusing on the exhaling breath, to enter and leave the Rainbow Garden (see Chapter 16 – summary of strategies). It was explained to her that as she became aware of uncomfortable feelings rising she could use the calming controlled breathing to keep focused. As silence became less threatening, her need for constant noise decreased and periods of extended working became easier.

Impact on family

Ella's adoptive parents were pleased to be able to relax their vigilance as she stopped putting anything and everything into her mouth. They were able to use the phrase, 'two small helpings of food' successfully at mealtimes at home encouraging her not to take too much food at once. The sayings and songs that Ella learnt at Wellie Wednesday helped her to control her impulsivity. Playing and learning with other children who had difficulties was helpful. Wellie Wednesday enabled her to experience the benefits of cooperating positively with her peers and she developed a calmer and more positive attitude.

Changes noticed in Ella

Emotional literacy work taught Ella that feelings and behaviour are different and that although feelings can often occur unpredictably, they can usually be contained by using good thinking to override any 'NOT OK' behaviour.

When Mr E praises other people I feel sad. Sometimes he gives me a wink or a high five sign. I know really he praises each person.

Ella had been able to feel sad but realised that her class teacher was not ignoring her, just ensuring that others got some of his attention too. Teaching her that jealous was perhaps the sad feeling she was experiencing, expanded her vocabulary of feelings. Once again, she was reassured that jealousy is a natural feeling experienced by everyone at times, but actions against another person or to divert attention to herself were not acceptable behaviours resulting from feeling jealous. Continuing to use and encourage all members of the group to use 'I feel …' language helped Ella to hear adults and children expressing how different situations made them feel. She became aware that the same event could cause different feelings, for example, a food loved by some people may not be loved by others if it was not their favourite food (see Chapter 15). Going to see the sheep caused great excitement for her but made some people feel nervous.

Ella relished drama sessions, so knowing how much she loved to act provided a good way for her to explore how others might feel. On a team member's follow-up visit to school Ella was asked to pretend to be her class teacher, and this allowed her to think about herself from a different perspective. The conversation went as follows:

TEAM MEMBER: Hello Mrs L, thank you for finding time to come and talk to me today, I was wondering how Ella is getting on in your class?

ELLA: Well sometimes Ella can be jumpy and over reactive but she is settling down. I'd like her to be a little calmer.

TEAM MEMBER: What does Ella do well?

ELLA: I've seen her drawing well, she gets loads of writing done but it's small. I really want bigger writing to be easier for my eyes to read.

TEAM MEMBER: Anything else?

ELLA: I am pleased when she gets on with her work and is calm.

TEAM MEMBER: How is she managing to do that do you think? (This question allowed Ella to focus on her success and think about how she gets it right.)

ELLA: She is listening to her parents more I think.

TEAM MEMBER: What else is she getting right in your class?

ELLA: Taking turns is important in my class. That is fair Ella thinks.

TEAM MEMBER: How is she now she is in year 4?

ELLA: She is tall, responsible, shares, doesn't tell lies, these are all year 4 things. In year 3 her work was scribbly now it is getting tidier.

TEAM MEMBER: That sounds as if Ella is doing well in your class.

ELLA: Yes I think Ella is pleased to be in my class.

TEAM MEMBER: How can you tell?

ELLA: Because of her happy face.

It was not necessary to confirm or deny what was said with the class teacher. The purpose of the role play was to allow Ella to think about what behaviour worked (or might work).

Conversations with children, asking them to reflect on what worked, how they did something well or how they know they are getting it right help to focus on the positive. By doing this we are reinforcing the desired behaviour so the child is better able to repeat it. Sometimes, if a child is struggling, the emphasis needs to be on how it would look if they were getting it right, and what would they be doing differently if things were going well (see solution focused – Chapter 18).

The concept of 'is it worth it?' was helpful for Ella in her dealings with peers. Children who often find themselves in trouble for retaliating feel hard done by, resulting in their sulking, unkind words or even hitting out. Thinking about the consequences of these actions helps children to recognise that to avoid trouble (i.e. 'keep Trouble out', see Chapter 10), sometimes it is best to shrug their shoulders with a deep breath (physically calming actions) and say to themselves: 'Is it worth it?' Ella thought this was worth a try and the following week her good news was:

> At the weekend I got really annoyed with my friend. I was going to hurt her then I thought, 'Is it worth it?' Then I felt proud.

Another time she recounted:

> When I went to L's house we took her dog for a walk. I walked it to the bandstand and then it was her turn all the way back. She wanted to hold it all the way back and it was very windy. It felt nice that I let her have a longer go even if it was unfair … she had longer. I said to myself that was good of me and it is her dog.

Transferring learning into school

At school Ella was given a specially designed chewing aid (Ps and Qs, www.sensetoys. com) to use. In a follow up meeting she raised the subject of why babies suck and chew things. This gave a good opportunity for explaining that babies need to explore what things are like but they have limited options compared with children, who can move about independently, speak and use thinking to work things out. As babies grow into these other ways they no longer need to explore with their mouths in the same way. In this way, Ella was able to hear that sucking and chewing non-food items are behaviours that do not need to last indefinitely.

Where entrenched behaviour is causing a child anguish, our message was always to reassure and empower them to believe 'change for the better' can happen. Ella had understood the message inherent in Crunch the Croc's story and became engaged in overcoming her similar habit. The puppet crocodile sought help for his problem behaviour, which was that his beautiful set of teeth was getting him into trouble because he just couldn't help using them to bite and chew anything he came across. No reference was made to the story having a parallel but it was no surprise that Ella wanted to see Crunch the Croc in the following weeks. Later in school at a follow-up meeting she said:

When I put things in my mouth I thought of Crunch and think, 'OOPs I shouldn't be putting that in my mouth but I can have my chewy thing instead.'

Sensory integration information was given to her parents, giving ideas of how Ella could experience some additional chewing, sucking and licking as it seemed possible she was having difficulties moving on from earlier developmental stages (see www.sensoryinfo.com/ResourcesPage.html for a wealth of fun sensory experiments for children).

Ashley, who also constantly wanted to put things in his mouth, was helped by using a water bottle, which required a lot of sucking to get the drink out. At home he was given thick milkshake in a drinking bottle to provide more of that sensory experience.

Another child, Zak, was allowed to have pieces of rusk, like crispbreads, in his desk to use instead of the paper clips, Blu-Tack and other items he had previously chewed. Once he had this option available he gradually ceased his old behaviour.

Chewy cereal bars cut up into pieces, along with crisp apple, carrot and celery sticks given as snacks, ensure plenty of chewing, crunching and sucking were all experienced. Blowing bubbles was also a popular activity and requires exercise for the muscles of the mouth. Consideration of earlier developmental needs was always an underlying factor in our choice of activities so that those whose early experiences had been limited could have an opportunity for second-chance learning (Winnicott 1964).

It seems that by giving reassurance that a behaviour can change, this can sometimes be enough to soothe the accompanying anxiety and thus reduce the need for the behaviour. A gradual retraining is often required for long-standing habits as there is unlikely to be a quick fix. However, once the behaviour has become an established habit rather than an anxiety-induced response, then simple reminders and praise for remembering are all that is needed to reinforce the change. Ella felt proud when she was able to use nice pencils because she no longer destroyed them with her excessive chewing. They served as a reminder of her successful change for the better.

Ella has been in school full-time since the project, with no exclusions. She sings in the choir and loves acting in a drama group. She has been extremely well-supported in school and has coped with changes of year group and staff. Ella has demonstrated how family, school and child working together can create a workable present and an optimistic future despite a difficult past.

Key strategies used

- Building trust.
- The use of non-verbal communication.
- Being kept in mind, not being forgotten.
- Transitional objects and time charts.

- Making friends with silence and stillness-soothing reassuring strategies.
- Rainbow garden visualisation.
- Silent speech bubble.
- Hare's listening ears.
- Focus on positive behaviour.
- 'Is it worth it?'
- Role play with herself as the teacher.

Reflection

What are the differences between attention seeking and attention needing? Does the terminology elicit a different response to meeting a child's needs?

References

Geddes, H. (2006). *Attachment in the classroom: The links between children's early experience, emotional wellbeing and performance in school*. London: Worth Publishing.
Winnicott, D.W. (1964). *The child, the family and the outside world*. London: Pelican Books.
Winnicott, D.W. (1971). *Playing and reality*. London: Routledge.

Chapter 8

Ned

Persevering pays off

> I get loads right now. Yesterday when Mrs D saw my mum through the window she gave her a thumbs up.
>
> (Ned)

Referral concerns from school and home

- Ned acts impulsively without thinking of the consequences.
- Ned gets up suddenly for no apparent reason, frequently knocking over his chair or jogging his neighbour in his haste.
- He bumps into others when moving about or lining up, causing his peers to make accusations of being hurt by him.
- He is impatient so instead of listening to instructions rushes to start saying 'I know, I know'.
- He becomes easily frustrated and gives up as soon as there is any need to think things through. Then he agrees to others taking over.
- He seeks for his mother to do things for him and gets irritated with her when she tries to help him, using disrespectful language towards her.
- Ned is unaware of the impact he has on others who are wary of his size and clumsiness.
- He pays little attention to turn taking and seems to see things only from his point of view.
- At home, when upset, he has been known to hold his breath for prolonged periods.
- He alienates and irritates some adults although in a one-to-one situation can converse with ease and good humour.
- He can sulk and refuse if he fails to get his own way or is told about mistakes he has made.
- He cannot easily sit with a still body to listen with attention. This appears at times to frustrate him as he struggles to stay focused, even on a subject that interests him.
- He overeats, always wanting more.

Ned's strengths as seen by the team

- Deep sensitivity and ability to empathise.
- Was keen to be involved.

- Liked practical activities.
- Wanted to problem-solve.
- Enjoyed being active.
- Liked music and wanted to learn the guitar.
- Enjoyed talking to adults, for example, about how things worked.
- A good sense of fun.

Understanding and making sense of concerns raised

Ned's referral information from school suggested that staff found him irritating and difficult to manage, describing his behaviour as rough, rather grumpy and sometimes rude. However, the list of concerns pointed to a lively impulsive child. His size created an image of an older child but in fact he was young for his school year and he joined the group full of impulsive enthusiasm.

He seemed to need and have some difficulties with physical activity. He wanted to be active and engage in sport but his poor coordination led to frustration. His rough exterior hid the inner sensitive character who was trying to be tough. He bottled up a lot of worries and deep concerns and when these became unmanageable they would emerge as intolerance and disruptive behaviour. Ned was a coper who tried to manage on his own. His teachers may have found it easier to deal with had he been distressed and in obvious need of comfort and support. It seemed that he was going to need help to deal with the cares he carried instead of only being able to display them through negative behaviour. When Ned did not get his own way he would sulk and see it as a sign that 'Everyone hates me'. This was an expression of how vulnerable he felt about himself and his ability to be liked.

Away from the confines of the classroom Ned was an endearing character. He did not seem to be an aggressive boy but wanted to engage with his peers, albeit over excitedly. This was well demonstrated when another child was opting out and he voluntarily paid her a compliment to draw her back into the group. Another time other children had been playfully throwing grass at an adult who asked them to stop. Ned had not joined in and quickly moved in to start picking off the individual strands of grass.

Ned was always quick to show enthusiasm but this would frequently turn to frustration. He then looked to his mum and demandingly expected her to take over for him. He was not open to the idea of being shown how to persevere and return to the task. Whenever things were a struggle for him he wanted to give up and have it done for him. He saw our preferred method of the adults offering to help children but not do it for them as evidence of his belief that 'No-one likes me' or he would utter his most frequent cry of 'It's not fair'. He swung between two extremes: the initial 'I can do this, I know how' and as soon as any real effort was required, 'I can't do it, you do it.' We needed to find ways to help his mum encourage and support him to persist.

Ned's perceived needs and individual targets

- To develop thinking skills to counter impulsivity.
- To realise he is likeable.

- To learn the social skills required for him to show friendly behaviour towards his peers.
- To have good quality fun time with his mother (understandably at home his disabled brother required a lot of attention).
- To use respectful language towards his mother.
- To build independence and not always expect his mother to take over.
- To investigate possible causes for his lack of physical coordination and clumsiness.
- To practise use of controlled movement, for example, balancing, coordination, as well as plenty of gross motor activity to enjoy the sense of space.
- To develop fine motor control skills, for example, to use a knife and fork to eat with and cut up his own food.
- To accept an appropriate amount of food to eat by taking a small portion at first and having a second helping if he still felt hungry.
- To accept mistake-making, to persevere through difficulty.
- To acknowledge intrinsic reward, and overcome his continual unsatisfying search for possessions and rewards.
- To recognise feelings of pride in his achievements.

In addition, as we got to know Ned it became apparent that he needed help to cope with normal sibling rivalries but in the difficult situation of feeling guilty because of his younger brother's disabilities.

Strategies used by the team to support Ned's needs

Building perseverance

Ned needed to gain a sense of achievement through successful persistence; he needed to learn perseverance through doing practical tasks, craft activities and physical challenges. By engaging in enjoyable tasks in which he wanted to succeed, he could experience the rewards of achieving what had at first seemed too difficult. Small steps were praised to recognise his efforts, encourage and keep him on task, for example, when balancing and walking along logs he was told: 'Well done Ned, you got half way, see if you can "beat your record" this time.'

He was also introduced to the Wellie Wednesday catch phrase:

> I can't do it YET
> But if I TRY MY BEST
> and
> PRACTISE
> soon I will be able to say
> I CAN.

Instead of giving up, Ned persevered and proudly showed one of the team how he could balance on the log walkway. Ned was then able to apply the same perseverance when he approached other tasks that at first seemed too difficult.

> At breakthrough moments, the team members would ask, 'How did you manage that?' This requires the child to mentally recall and put into words their effective strategy, for example, 'I didn't give up' or 'I said I can't do it YET and had another go' or 'First I got half way then I got further' or 'I practised'. This self-talk encourages them to see themselves as successful at sticking to a task until it is satisfactorily accomplished.

Supporting and building independence

Activities were introduced where there was no right or wrong way to do something, for example, to create a small world in a sand tray. The children were given an individual small tray of sand and a wealth of small items to arrange in any way they wished. With no pressure on needing a particular outcome, Ned was able to settle into deep concentration. Parents and carers were asked to watch, i.e. give undivided attention but not to comment, suggest or join in. When Ned undertook this task he learnt that support did not have to mean having it done for him. His mother also learnt how hard she found it not to take over!

Other parents and carers, too, learnt that often what children need is not to have things done for them but rather the support and encouragement of being present as their child attempts a challenging task. They found that learning to positively commentate brought remarkable changes in their child's ability to persevere, stay focused and withstand frustration. Such non-judgemental comments as 'I can see you are concentrating hard', 'I like the way you decided how to do that', 'I saw you thinking hard about which colour would look best' help a child to keep going with a task and shape their behaviour towards achieving a successful outcome.

Developing thinking skills: 'Think before you say/do'

How do I know what I think until I hear myself say it?

(George Brown, MP)

For the naturally impulsive, having a strategy to help restrain that impulsivity is helpful in giving themselves time to stop and think before acting or reacting. Ned was helped to understand that better results come from planning, thinking and mental rehearsal. Sayings and songs were used to reinforce developing these cognitive skills, i.e. 'Think before you do', 'Think before you say'. It seemed impossible for Ned to hold ideas and thoughts in his head and he was frequently in trouble for calling out and interrupting. Our thinking song was used to familiarise the children with the concept of restraining their urge to blurt out what they were thinking or to do things without forethought:

Just a minute, let me think
Let me think, let me think.
Just a minute, let me think
Think before I say.

Just a minute, let me think
Let me think, let me think.
Just a minute, let me think
Think before I do.

(sung to the tune of "London Bridge is falling down")

Once the song was learnt, 'think before you say' was used to encourage the children to spend a minute using 'thinking time' before being asked to contribute answers or ideas. For Ned, the urgency to get his say first subsided as he learnt that everyone would get a turn and it was not a race to be first to speak. This was reinforced by praise for 'good waiting' addressed to the child who had waited to make the final contribution.

Developing thinking skills: rewind

When Ned acted impulsively a reminder was given, 'Remember, think before you do' and then he was asked to 'rewind', to go back to where he had been and try again. The essence of this strategy was not about being punitive because he had got something wrong, but it was done to encourage reflection alongside support, humour and praise for getting it right on a second attempt, for example, after he had acted impulsively: 'Whoops Ned, I think that needs a rewind.' By repeating an action correctly, rather than only giving a verbal explanation or reprimand, it is then better embedded (through the physical and mental action) and has a far greater chance of being repeated in the future.

Developing thinking skills: mistake making

Ned, burdened with anxieties and vulnerabilities, could not cope with being wrong. It was as if admitting to any mistake, however small, would serve to add to his negative self-image. His method of coping was to deny the mistakes and wrongdoings to himself as much as to others. When a child is unable to accept being in the wrong it is often a sign that they are in need of praise and building a sense of themselves as being generally successful. Once success and praise are in place a mistake is not such a big issue because the cushion of feelings of self-worth can absorb it.

A card with these words on was seen above a workplace desk:

I learnt so much from the last mistake I made that I think I will make another.

Instead of seeing mistakes as wilful acts of disobedience or defiance the team used them as examples of areas where a child needed guidance. 'What isn't taught isn't learnt' is the case for many children, especially those with specific learning difficulties. Some children have learnt to feel that mistakes are irretrievable disasters, usually as a result of:

- An over developed sense of competition where 'winning' is paramount and admission of error is seen as weakness.
- Having been frequently punished in response to both real and perceived wrongdoing.
- Having difficulty coping with any negative experiences that would add to their already unworthy or unlovable sense of self.

Fear of being in the wrong, dread of punishment and an overwhelming sense of failure, can lead to defensiveness, denial of wrongdoing and telling lies.

Developing thinking skills: Check and change

In order to remove the stigma, anxiety and distress caused by making mistakes, 'check and change' was taught. This meant to check the last thing that was done, said or written and think how to change it for the better. A toy chameleon, Charlie Change, was used to introduce the groups to the idea. Adults, too, found themselves using check and change not only with the children but for themselves (adapted to incorporate behaviour from *Top Ten Thinking Tactics*, Lake and Needham 1995).

Children were praised for changing their minds, stopping what they were doing that wasn't working and trying a different method, for example: 'Well done for check and change. I saw you think about carrying too many sticks and deciding to do it in two loads.' The phrase was learnt first as a form of praise and then it could be applied when mistakes were made without causing distress.

When Ned overstepped the mark playing with his peers he was given a quick reminder: 'Do you need to check and change, Ned? Was that kind?' Instead of denial he was quick to apologise: 'Sorry mate, are you OK?' When he had snatched something from another child he was asked: 'Was that kind, Ned? Can you check and change?' He replied: 'Sorry, you had it first.' In this case he was then encouraged to say: 'Can I have a turn with it next please?' This helped him to learn a useful script for future use instead of relying on actions first. By reducing Ned's need to be right at all costs, his good humour emerged he started to demonstrate a playfulness with other children.

Target chart

In school, Ned had a small copy of the 'getting it right' target chart on his desk. This had all the 'getting it right targets' printed onto it around the symbol of the Wise Turtle. These small achievable aims helped to remind Ned that even if the work was proving difficult, he could still be doing good sitting, good thinking, good waiting, good listening and good following instructions.

Silent speech bubble

His teacher placed a 'silent speech bubble' on the wall at the front of the classroom. When Ned was chatting to others at inappropriate times or calling out the teacher pointed to it providing a non-verbal reminder to Ned. A voices song was introduced to build understanding of using different voices in different situations. Ned was encouraged to use his thinking voice when he was not supposed to be talking.

Voices (said using the appropriate voice, children can add others)

Have you brought your whispering voices?
Yes we have. Yes we have.

Have you brought your speaking voices?
Yes we have. Yes we have.

Have you brought your squeaky voices?
Yes we have. Yes we have.

Have you brought your growly voices?
Yes we have. Yes we have.

Have you brought your thinking voices?
(say it in your head nodding only) Yes we have. Yes we have.

(J. Pitt[1])

Ned found it helpful to have a small tortoise who he called Robbie Remember in his desk. This linked to the Hope Family used to teach about the Wellie Wednesday targets. When Ned opened his desk he felt encouraged to 'get it right'.

I see Robbie Remember and think, don't get sent out. I stay in and give myself a thumbs up.

Recognising feelings of pride

A tortoise character called Princess Proud was used to help the children identify what it feels like to experience success. Successful outcomes are often praised, for example, a well-drawn picture or a completed task. However, in order to develop a child's self-image, there is an additional need to praise the underlying attributes and skills required to achieve those end results, for example, attention to detail when drawing, concentration until finished, following the instructions accurately.

Princess Proud and her friends, including Percy Persevere, Patience, Charlie Change and Try My Best, helped the children to recognise their own efforts and feel good about times when they overcame difficult feelings or situations. These intrinsic rewards are the building blocks of a positive self-image. Extrinsic rewards should serve as stepping stones to identifying the intrinsic value of achievement. Ned's driving search for external possessions and rewards diminished as he became aware of the benefits that sharing, cooperation, fun and creativity could bring.

> The children were encouraged to feel proud of their achievements and this helped them to increase their understanding of self-control. They were taught when they felt proud to acknowledge this feeling and praise themselves. Signs were developed that children could use unobtrusively in school, for example, with hands under their desks giving a thumbs up or a silent clap with finger and thumb together. Taking time to experience feelings of pride was encouraged in order to make them aware and to anchor the positive feeling for mentally revisiting later.
>
> When they had achieved success they were asked: 'What did you do that made you feel proud of yourself?' Every opportunity was used for the children to verbalise how they had been successful and how it made them feel. Putting these feelings and their successful strategies into words allowed them to hear themselves describing their own success and so transformed their previously held poor self-beliefs.
>
> Photographs were used to illustrate their successes and were given to them as visual reminders of their 'can do' moments. These moments and their associated photographs became powerful inspirations. One group took up the idea with a 'Proud Wall'. A child who overcame fear and managed to climb a tree was given a photograph of himself being brave. He continued to use his 'I did it' experience to encourage himself to have a go at other things he found difficult. At the end of the year he looked at his photograph and asked his teacher to keep it. He said: 'I don't need it now, I remember I did it.'

Impact on the family

At home, Ned and his mother benefited from setting aside one to one time each week for cooking and eating a meal together after his brother was in bed. They enjoyed continuing the Wellie Wednesday activities at home. His mother noticed that he joined in with pleasure rather than grumbling 'I'm bored'. Some of Ned's favourites were using salt dough, making habitats for imaginary creatures and creating a tent-like den as his 'special place' in his bedroom. His good news was:

> I don't call my mum an idiot any more, now I say 'I love you' to her.

> Another mother took up the 'special place' idea for her two children by giving them a tiny tent each on the landing as their own special place. Despite sharing a small bedroom, and previously having had numerous and frequent arguments, they enjoyed having their own space and respected each other's need for privacy and quiet times.

By having some special times together with his mother, Ned's constant demands reduced. As he became more confident in his own abilities he started to enjoy rather than be frustrated by challenges.

> I looked for my book. I didn't want to ask Mum to find it. I wanted to find it myself.

Ned's mother was introduced to a parent support worker who was able to enrol Ned in after school activities to help his coordination and give him the extended physical challenges that she found difficult to offer because of her commitments to her younger child. Ned thrived on swimming and martial arts training, both of which helped not only physically but by continuing to channel his energy constructively, developing his concentration and improving his self-control.

Cooking and eating together and having a sharing plate of cut-up food helped Ned to see food preparation as a fun part of sociable eating. He enjoyed the serving and conversations as well as the food. From his usual stance of always claiming to be hungry, wanting to pile his plate high but then not eating it all, he moved to enjoying being given a small helping with the assurance there would be a second helping if he wanted one. His mother found she could use this strategy successfully at home as well.

Ned and his mother became less confrontational with each other through the emphasis on kindness that permeated the Wellie Wednesday project.

Our belief 'We are kind to each other' was recited and demonstrated repeatedly within the group. Kindness was explicitly taught with regard to the wildlife. Attention was paid to replacing insects after looking at them, removing insects gently from the tents, not pulling up plants or breaking twigs off trees, and moving slowly and quietly around the animals. Kind actions were always noticed and remarked upon: 'Well done for remembering to be kind to ...'

The children were asked to handle the puppets and animal characters with care. The children experienced frequent examples of gentleness and kindness and were reminded that their own brain benefits from such experiences. It is known that the response to kindness is a release of oxytocin by both the giver and receiver thereby nurturing mutual feelings of well-being. To demonstrate this effect, a piece of carbon paper was used to represent the brain of another person with the under sheet representing their own brain. The word KINDNESS was then written on the top sheet and handed to someone else to symbolise doing something kind for them. To their surprise when the underneath sheet was revealed the word KINDNESS was clearly imprinted on it. Conversely acts of aggression cause adrenalin levels to rise, creating confrontational feelings of anxiety, restlessness and anger in both the giver and receiver.

Changes noticed in Ned

Recognising feelings

Learning the difference between feelings, thoughts and behaviour and that thoughts can be helpful or unhelpful gave Ned the tools he needed to help deal with the frustrations he was experiencing.

It was important for Ned to learn to moderate his 'all or nothing' polarised thinking. Teaching Ned to better understand his feelings using the 'Feelings Thermometer' (Greenburg and Kusche 1995) helped him to understand that emotions can be felt at different levels, for example, cross, annoyed, angry, furious, OK, fine, content, delighted, joyful, happy. He was able to apply this increasing vocabulary of emotions in order to better recognise his feelings so instead of saying 'Everyone hates me', he was able to say 'I feel annoyed because …'. As soon as Ned started to use 'I feel …' language, the team were quick to acknowledge this with: 'It's OK to feel annoyed when it's not your turn Ned, but it can't always be your turn first.'

Children seem to cope much better when they have their feelings named: 'I can see that you feel disappointed that Sam doesn't want to play with you at the moment.' 'I realise you don't feel like putting your boots on but you know that to go into the woods you need to wear boots.'

I thinked in my head – I didn't throw things about – I didn't be mad. I did feel mad.

At a follow-up meeting, Ned started a conversation about exploding fireworks. The following week he said 'I'm keeping my anger inside by stopping and not exploding.' He then drew an exploded and an unexploded firework with his Robbie Remember Tortoise beside them. He said the exploded one was a celebration firework for keeping anger from exploding. He had transferred his talk of an unexploded firework into his understanding of being angry and this had enabled him to change the way he responded to the feeling. It was interesting that he saw Robbie Remember as part of his success. He also said: 'Princess Proud says "Well done Ned"'. Then he added: 'I say to my sister sometimes "I feel angry so keep away", nothing has been thrown this week.' By expressing his feeling his older sister had been able to move away and give him space to calm down.

Adults, too, benefited from a better understanding of the importance of acknowledging feelings but separating them from behaviours. One mother told us she was amazed when she tried this with one of her teenage daughters and said, 'All I said was it must feel annoying that you can't find the shoes you want to wear but you must leave now or you will be late for school.' It had been known for such instances to result in refusal to go to school. This time to her mother's amazement her daughter put on another pair and ran off calling out, 'Bye Mum, love you'. The mother said previously she would have got involved in a prolonged argument over such an issue, shouting comments such as 'You are going to be late for school', 'You must look for it yourself', 'You should look after your things and know where they are.' These had only served to entrench the daughter's position and escalate her defiant behaviour. This time instead, her mother acknowledging and showing she understood her feelings, had acted to calm her so she could act rationally.

Ned used the creative visualisation we called the Rainbow Garden for self-calming. Ned explained: 'I go to the Rainbow Garden loads at night, it helps me to sleep. When my brother is not being nice to me I go into my bedroom and under my duvet to the Rainbow Garden.'

Knowing he was being heard, having his own special one to one time at home and at school, learning new motor skills, being given some responsibilities and at times being the one who made the choices was enough to allow Ned to cope better with the constraints of classroom and family life. Successful completion of Wellie Wednesday tasks and experiencing the satisfaction of achievement helped him to understand that the same was required of his school work. 'Beating his record' for the number of sums or amount of writing allowed him to view these challenges in a positive non-threatening light, resulting in a more focused effort and greater accomplishment. In Ned's own words: 'I get loads right now. Yesterday when Mrs D saw my mum through the window she gave her a thumbs up.'

Transferring learning into school

A daily 'meet and greet' session was set up for Ned with the school counsellor, which provided time every morning for Ned to chat, practise some balancing and coordination exercises and make the transition from home into school. At times, Ned also benefited from longer sessions where he was given freedom to choose his activity, i.e. he was in control. During these times, the conversations he initiated showed his deep sensitivity and ability to empathise, traits previously not apparent to those trying to help him.

He was also able to use his special one to one time in school to explore his ambivalent feelings, especially his outbursts when his younger sibling caused him to feel deeply frustrated but also guilty that he was failing in his role as the big brother. He would say: 'But my brother is little and disabled.' Allowing Ned to know that all siblings get frustrated with each other at times and to remember that 'all feelings are OK but our behaviour can be OK or NOT OK' helped him to handle his conflicting feelings. This was combined with teaching him 'good ignoring' tactics, i.e. practising moving away (instead of retaliating). He did remarkably well at practising this and it is to his credit that he preferred the outcome when he removed himself rather than escalating a disagreement. He told us of a time when his brother was annoying him: 'I felt angry with my brother so I kept away, I think Princess Proud says: "Well done Ned."'

Key strategies used

- Building perseverance.
- Encouraging independence.
- Developing thinking skills:
  - 'Think before you do.'
  - Rewind.
  - Mistake making.
  - 'Check and change.'
- Target chart to identify success.
- Silent speech bubble.

- Understanding and managing feelings and behaviour.
- Building in one-to-one time.
- Recognising feelings of pride.

Reflection

How does physical clumsiness impact upon a child's classroom and playground experiences? What forms of differentiation could help? How can school help with the impact on a pupil of having a sibling at home with a severe disability?

Note

1 Pitt, J., Tutor MA early years music at Centre for Research in Early Childhood; Visiting lecturer, University of Roehampton.

References

Greenberg, M. and Kusche, C. (1995). *Promoting alternative thinking strategies (PATHS)*. South Deerfield: Channing-Bete.
Lake, M. and Needham, M. (1995). *Top ten thinking tactics: A practical introduction to the thinking skills revolution*. Birmingham: Imaginative Minds.

Introduction to the case studies

Addressing concerns

> While we are together, let us think about not just who you are now but who you would like to be in the future.
>
> (Sarah Rockliff)

Many children who have experienced trauma in their early life communicate their distress through their behaviour. The following chapters illustrate some of these behaviours and the ways of working that were developed to support them.

A high proportion of the children who took part in the Wellie Wednesday project were considered vulnerable at that time. Many had experienced difficult attachment situations and in some cases had experienced bereavement or separation from parents or siblings. Some were living with step-parents, some had been fostered, some were adopted and some were cared for by grandparents. For some children, violence and uncertainty had been part of their early lives.

The following chapters demonstrate how challenging behaviour can be a means of communicating distressing feelings. Within this safe environment, children were able to learn alternative and more positive ways to be themselves. It is hoped that these chapters will provide ideas and ways forward for others.

> Children need to be themselves, to live with other children and with grown-ups, to learn from their environment, to enjoy the present, to get ready for the future, to create and to love, to learn to face adversity, to behave responsibly, in a word to be human beings.
>
> (Plowden report, Central Advisory Council for Education. *Children and their Primary Schools*, HMSO 1967)

Chapter 9

Language and communication skills
What is special about Shaun?

> I realise he's not being as naughty as I think he is.
>
> (Shaun's mother said to his teacher)

Pen picture of Shaun

Shaun joined the project as one of our youngest children. At school, he was experiencing difficulties, especially with his concentration and his poor language development. His parents saw him as the 'problem child' in their family. The problems they were experiencing were those of an impulsive little boy, vying for attention with a baby and an older, more competent brother. Sibling rivalry and arguments quickly became fights with his brother, who was stronger and better equipped to justify himself verbally. For Shaun, expressing himself in words was frequently too slow and frustrating, so at home and at school he lived by an 'actions speak louder than words' policy.

Participating in Wellie Wednesday gave Shaun's mother the chance to spend a whole day focused on Shaun. It was a wonderful opportunity for them to enjoy being together. Shaun was delighted; he arrived beaming from ear to ear, the smile rarely leaving his face over the next few weeks. Whatever difficulties he met, he made up for with enthusiasm and good humour.

Shaun was overly affectionate towards the adults, wanting to hug people he had only just met. This was not unique to Shaun; a number of the children exhibited this overly familiar behaviour. Whilst it can be seen as endearing, we wanted to discourage indiscriminate affection in favour of developing meaningful relationships and fostering a deeper bond between parents or carers and children.

Learning about communication

Building relationships and awareness of personal space

At the start of the day, the children, parents and carers were greeted as they got off the bus using handshakes. This introduced an appropriate form of touch that could also be used on follow-up visits in school. As familiarity and affection grew, Shaun was taught to use a 'sideways hug', where the adult standing beside him would put an arm around his shoulders using a supportive squeeze whilst maintaining safe personal space. The concept of 'personal space' was taught by describing it as an imaginary bubble around each person. The children were then told to 'Remember, to keep each others' personal space safe' when they were inappropriately touching another, for example, tugging them, sitting too close or pushing. Praise was given each time Shaun remembered to respect another's personal space by sitting alongside but without touching.

Understanding, interpreting and following instructions

Shaun's difficulties with processing language were a frequent cause of misunderstanding and inability to remember what he was supposed to be doing.

In cognitive terms, there are three phases in successfully processing information (Feuerstein and Rand 1977): *input* involves holding received information in working memory; *elaboration* involves comprehending and interpreting information, for example, in order to interpret an instruction; *output* requires further word processing in order to respond. Failure in any one of these stages will result in the same outcome but the cause will be different. Establishing which is the area of weakness is allows for focus on the correct form of remediation. A further explanation can be found in an overview of Feuerstein's work, *Changing Children's Minds* (Sharron and Coulter 1996).

In Shaun's case, the input and elaboration phases were weak. In a desperate effort to please, he would hurtle into action when he had grasped only part of what was required. Sadly, half the information is rarely enough for a good outcome. Sure enough, when he realised that he did not know what to do, he would either come to a grinding halt or he would carry on doing what he guessed had been wanted. Either of these responses resulted in his mother being cross with him for not doing what she had wanted him to do. Similarly his teacher was frustrated by his seeming lack of focus on listening in order to follow her instructions.

'Take up time' and time warnings

'Take up time' was introduced. As words are said (input) a child needs to be able to absorb and interpret them (elaboration) before acting on them (output). Sometimes, when children do not respond instantaneously, it is assumed that they are disobeying. Parents and carers were encouraged to practise counting slowly and silently to ten before repeating an instruction. They were frequently amazed to find that by giving 'take up time' they had not only been heard but also obeyed. If a follow-up instruction was required, they learnt to repeat the same wording prefaced by saying the child's name. Sometimes there is a temptation to rephrase the instruction but introducing new vocabulary confuses a child who has weak auditory or processing skills. By repeating the same wording, the child can continue processing the same instruction.

Time warnings were also used to allow children to wind down from an activity, for example, 'in five minutes it will be tidy up time'. Adults were able to transfer this strategy to home where they could use it for bedtimes and mealtimes. This was also useful for children who had difficulty changing activities.

'Think before I say' and 'think before I do'

Shaun seemed to have developed his own strategy for allowing processing time as he prefaced every answer, comment or question with the words 'only because'. He said this slowly, providing himself with thinking time as he worked on what he wanted to say.

We taught all the children to give themselves thinking time before speaking. Whenever a question was asked, no answers were accepted before a short 'Think before you speak' time had elapsed. These moments make all the difference to the quality of answer and the number of children who could contribute. The first priority for Shaun was to slow down so that he could use 'Think before I speak'.

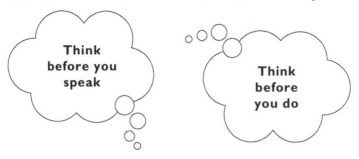

Clear concise instruction and clarification

The second priority was helping his mum not to bombard him with words but to give clear concise instructions and an expectation that Shaun would follow them.

In order to help develop Shaun's memory he would be asked to repeat what he had to do. If he seemed uncertain, he would be asked: 'What is it you need to be doing now?' If he could not answer this question then he became aware of his lack of understanding. Some children are simply not aware that they do not understand.

If life makes little sense, if cause and effect are not concepts you have experienced, and if routines are lacking, then much of what is heard and expected is incomprehensible. Being asked 'Do you understand?' therefore also lacks meaning, but children who want to please will always answer 'yes' to this question. The use of 'What do you need to do?' was encouraged in place of 'Do you understand?' This requires the child to verbalise the required action. Repeating the instruction themselves increases the likelihood of them carrying out the action. Conversely, if they do not know what to do, when they become aware of this they begin to learn what 'understanding' feels like.

It was a heartening breakthrough moment when Shaun did not attempt to start an activity, saying instead: 'I don't know how to …'

Changes noticed in Shaun

When family life is busy and there are several siblings, being heard often requires shouting loudest or doing the most disruptive things to gain parental attention. Gaining a label within a family, for example, the naughty one, the chatty one, the loud one, the clever one, results in those qualities being most frequently noticed. Shaun's older, more able, brother had become quick to pass on blame and to attribute all misdeeds to him. For the parents of larger families who were able to attend Wellie Wednesday, focusing on one child was a treat. Shaun's mother delighted in seeing him differently as she watched his kindnesses to his peers, his helpfulness to staff and his excitement at sharing new experiences with her. She said to his teacher: 'I realise he's not being as naughty as I think he is.' The teacher saw change in Shaun and his mother as they attended Wellie Wednesday and began to experience things differently.

His mother found she could incorporate much of what she had learnt into home life. During a follow-up visit to school she made the following observations:

- Shaun has started laying the table and showing his brothers how to get their own breakfast.
- I don't shout back anymore. I stay more relaxed.
- He used to fall asleep after school even when he had friends round. We have a bedtime routine now before he gets over-tired, we use the Rainbow Garden visualisation (see Chapter 16).
- Now I give him a reason he can't do something and he calms down.
- I used to think he couldn't do things, like I used to cut up his food. Now I let him help me. He folds the laundry and helps cook; he never used to before Wellie Wednesday.
- I said I need to keep you safe and he holds hands to walk to school. No wrist strap anymore, it used to be a battle. Now he knows we need to keep him safe so he doesn't think it's a punishment anymore.
- If he needs to calm down I tell him 'time out' for one minute, his brother gets longer because he answers back but Shaun doesn't retaliate now.
- I used the shared fruit plate as an after school snack and it is a good time for my sons to get on well together.

In school Shaun was able to stand up each week to tell his peers what he had been doing on Wellie Wednesday. The teacher said the other children were excited by what they heard, and not jealous. So Shaun had moved from poor language skills to being able to hold his audience's attention with his descriptions and explanations of his days at Wellie Wednesday. He was also showing that he could transfer what he had learnt at Wellie Wednesday into school and home. For example, he said to his teacher: 'I remembered to do quiet listening when Joe was making a noise.'

Reflection

When a child ignores an instruction, could this indicate that they have not understood the language used by the adult? Do we allow enough 'take up' time for children to absorb and process a question or instruction before expecting them to respond?

References

Feuerstein, R. and Rand, Y. (1977). *Studies in cognitive modifiability instrumental enrichment: Redevelopment of cognitive functions.* Jerusalem: HWCRI.

Sharron, H. and Coulter, M. (1996). *Changing children's minds: Feuerstein's revolution in the teaching of intelligence.* Birmingham: Imaginative Minds.

Chapter 10

Narrative conversations to find solutions

What is special about Dillon?

All my life Angry has been fighting Good.
I will use Will Power to make the right choice.

(Dillon)

Pen picture of Dillon

Dillon was a highly anxious but deep-thinking child. His early experiences, which included ill health and loss within the family, had caused him stress and anxiety. His behaviour in school was challenging and had proved difficult to manage. Whereas some children use 'fight or flight' as their survival mechanisms, for Dillon, 'freeze' was more often the outcome of any potentially challenging situation. He frequently refused to move from one place to another. For example, on some days he would refuse to go out to play, but on days when he had managed to go out he would become 'stuck' over how to get back in. Staff struggled with his very challenging and disruptive behaviour. They tried rewards, consequences, cajoling, ignoring and sanctions.

Dillon's anxiety affected his eating; at times he would be physically sick before meals. These anxiety symptoms diminished over the weeks of the Wellie Wednesday project.

Dillon's main strength was that he was able to use his imagination. In the past, this skill caused him additional difficulties as he was able to imagine worst-case scenarios, which resulted in panic. At Wellie Wednesday he was able to find new ways to enjoy playfully using his imagination.

Another strength was his ability to communicate his worries using expressive language and an extensive vocabulary. He was very thoughtful, deeply caring and very sensitive. This enabled us to readily engage him in problem-solving conversations around his anxieties.

Reducing high anxiety

Reducing Dillon's anxiety was going to be a high priority but not easily achieved. The combination of his imagination and thinking caused him to readily project a pessimistic view of what the future might hold. His anxious manner and challenging behaviour inevitably drew adults into conflict situations with him.

Dillon needed to be given the opportunity for plenty of light-hearted and fun interactions, along with enjoyable sensory experiences, in order to help him overcome his deep-seated expectation that new meant scary. The experiences we provided for him were:

- Songs and rhymes with a positive message.
- Stories that featured creatures whose identifying characteristics were positive, for example, wisdom, hope, trust.
- Physical activities, including running and stopping at the sound of a whistle then carrying on. This gave him an enjoyable experience of freezing, then moving on swiftly.
- Bubble-blowing with running and jumping to catch them.
- Running and returning games, so 'coming back' could be experienced as part of a fun experience.

Narrative conversations – 'keeping Trouble out' – exploring helpful thinking

The approach of using externalizing conversations to personify the child's difficulties was inspired by the work of Alice Morgan (1999).

Dillon was encouraged to use his already well-established thinking and imagination to construct new ways of looking at his world. He was exposed to how others think by using animal characters who told their stories about how they dealt with change. Dillon named a new character 'Will Power', who showed determination in the face of adversity.

In addition, Dillon saw and heard other children dealing with uncomfortable feelings and challenging situations and noted how they were supported to make good choices and 'get it right'. Through these insights, the way was paved for Dillon to look at how he might like things to change for the better.

Conversations with Dillon encouraged him to externalise the difficulty, whatever he perceived it to be, then tease out how it caused him 'Trouble'. The emphasis was on looking for ways to 'keep Trouble out'.

Here, Dillon is exploring his thoughts and feelings with a team member:

DILLON: All my life Angry has been fighting Good.

This statement provided an opportunity for further questions to extend his thinking using his chosen terminology.

TEAM MEMBER: I wonder how you know when Angry is coming; what do you notice?

Wondering and noticing are useful investigative concepts, allowing the child to be reflective, rather than asking a direct question, which is more likely to elicit the response 'I don't know'.

DILLON: Ha Ha Ha Ha is the sound of Angry coming, I'll get you … I can get inside your body is what Angry says.

At this point Dillon was encouraged to explore what happens if 'Angry gets inside', then allowed responses.

TEAM MEMBER: So it sounds as if Angry causes you a lot of Trouble? If Angry is getting you into Trouble I wonder what it would be like if Angry wasn't around so much?

Different possible futures were explored:

TEAM MEMBER: I wonder how you could keep Angry and his friend Trouble out of your life? I wonder if there is anyone else who can help you to keep Angry out?
DILLON: Good is very nice … it likes little boys and little girls.

Dillon was now asked to explore how Good's 'helpful thinking' might help at times when he was feeling worried and Angry might find it easy to 'get into his body'. Dillon thought Good did have some helpers who he knew, he said they were God, Percy Persevere (the Hope Family tortoise who keeps trying even when it's difficult) and Miss S. (his teaching assistant).

Dillon's conversation had enabled him to explore ideas that:

- Identified strategies that helped him to feel calmer, for example, calming breathing, supportive rhymes or songs, positive role model characters.
- Externalised his difficulty with handling anger so he could explore what might help him.
- Provided emotional support for getting it right by feeling that Good was on his side and that he knew some of Good's helpers.

7/11 breathing

Dillon learnt the calming breathing technique called 7/11 breathing – inhale to the count of seven, exhale to the count of eleven (see Chapter 16) – and was encouraged to use it when he was worried. Miss S. said that she had seen him doing this at times in class. He also developed his own extension of the breathing exercise by using his fingers to count the 7/11, his hands moved together and apart, first vertically, then horizontally and finally diagonally. Dillon found that the concentration on executing the breathing and the movements helped him to keep control of his feelings. He also transferred other ideas to home and school. He told Miss S.: 'I do "balancing rainbows" even in the bath!' (making a rainbow arc with his arms in time with his breathing). At a follow-up meeting he said: 'I do the 7/11 breathing in the night time so I get to sleep better and 'the cross overs' in the morning to wake me up.' (see Chapter 16). He then went on to demonstrate how he could do the 7/11 movements even when lying down! He also said he liked going to the Rainbow Garden before going to sleep: 'The Rainbow Twins let me have tea with them, they eat fish and seaweed.' (see Chapter 16).

Feelings Scale

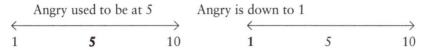

Angry used to be at 5   Angry is down to 1

| 1 | **5** | 10 | | **1** | 5 | 10 |

Using the Feelings Scale and Feelings Thermometer with Miss S. helped him to identify that feelings varied in intensity, and even when they were high ('up towards ten') it was possible for change to happen and the intensity could be reduced. By teaching a wider vocabulary of feelings, anger was seen as one of a number of uncomfortable feelings. When Dillon thought he was angry he came to realise that sometimes he was frustrated, annoyed, worried or upset and these feelings resulted in less disruptive behaviour.

Dillon told of a day when he had gone out to play at lunchtime: 'I wanted to play on the mound and I couldn't (it was time to go in). I felt I was going to get in an attitude and throw stones about. I told Angry to go away with my hand held up and then I picked up a stick and batted it up into space. I dropped the stick and went into school. I said "I have been good, I have hit Angry away and it can't get me any more".'

He also had a new insight: 'Trouble wants me to pretend I am not well and not go to assembly. Some days when I say "go away" it works and I go into assembly. Some days Trouble wins, then I sit near but not through the hall doors.' Staff agreed to his compromise.

Changing 'unhelpful thinking' to 'helpful thinking'

Awareness was raised about the difference between helpful and unhelpful thinking and how this can influence feelings and actions. An optimistic approach to the future, for example, 'the glass is half full', encouraged a more positive outlook even in challenging situations. Stories were used to illustrate this point, for example, *The Old Woman Who Lived in a Vinegar Bottle* who was always discontented.

Dillon would often say 'I don't want to' in response to a number of situations, particularly his dislike of following instructions. This provided an opportunity to explore helpful and unhelpful thinking and to talk about what was stopping him from getting it right:

TEAM MEMBER: Perhaps Don't Want is unhelpful? Can you think of a time when Don't Want was unhelpful?

DILLON: At playtimes when I follow instructions to go out but Don't Want wants me to stay in. At bedtime Don't Want keeps me up late.

TEAM MEMBER: So does Don't Want have to get her own way or can you choose to get it right and follow instructions?

DILLON (after some thought): I'll keep control by using my brain, and follow instructions. I'll use my Feelings Thermometer and if I think Don't Want is getting me into the red I'll say 'Just a minute, let me think' and I will use Will Power to make the right choice.

The following week Dillon had good news:

DILLON: Don't Want doesn't get what she wants to, for me not to go into assembly. I've been every time. When its playtime I say, 'I'm not listening to you Don't Want.'

He was then asked to think about what it was like being outside. This was in order to expand his positive thoughts about joining in.

DILLON: I was playing hide and seek with five friends: L, H, J, H and R.

The team member responded, encouraging Dillon to think about the feeling of fun.

TEAM MEMBER: That sounds as if Dillon got to have fun. What else did you do?
DILLON: Another day I played 'It'.
TEAM MEMBER: So that means that following instructions to go out to play can lead to fun. Perhaps you can meet Fun in the playground every day?
DILLON: When I go out to play friends ask me to play with them … when I go out to play I use my super brain.

Dillon concluded the meeting by once again extending an idea. From thinking about how to get into assembly and out to play by keeping Trouble out, he added a new plan:

DILLON: When work is hard, instead of Walk Away and Give Up, I am going to use Try My Best.

Changes noticed in Dillon

School staff found that it was helpful to use the terminology that Dillon had learnt at Wellie Wednesday. When Dillon was writing his sentences and he said 'I can't do it', Miss S. reminded him to 'try your best', then he went back to his work and finished it. On another occasion when he was getting annoyed, Miss S. reminded him that he can 'check and change' and she said that when he had finished he said that he felt proud. Dillon remembered another time when he didn't want to leave the computer to go to bed: 'then I thought check and change and so I did.'

Dillon demonstrated that memories of Wellie Wednesday had remained firmly fixed in his brain: months later he sent a message to the team: 'I like listening to the sounds and songs of Wellie Wednesday on the CD Jessica gave us, Grandad likes it too. I like the sound of the sizzly sausages cooking. Singing the "Just a minute, let me think" song helps. Thank you Jessica.'

Dillon continued to show increased confidence as he put into practice and extended, in his own individual and unique way, everything he had learnt at Wellie Wednesday. He was able to develop his thinking and gain support from the imaginary characters who had become a part of his life.

Chapter 11

Anxiety-driven behaviour

What is special about Elise?

> I turned uncomfortable into comfortable, doing something else can help with uncomfortable feelings.
>
> (Elise)

Pen picture of Elise

Elise had experienced the loss of parents and siblings in the early stages of her life. It seemed that silence was unbearable for her and so she disrupted quiet times. The unknown was anxiety-raising and intrusive thoughts filled her head if she allowed herself a moment's quiet. She kept up a constant internal conversation which spilled over into lengthy monologues. She asked numerous questions with no interest in listening to the answers. She was also skilled in coming up with innovative ideas to distract from the current task. She became distracted in some lessons more than others, even though the content was well within her capabilities.

At times Elise would bang her head with her fist, saying 'I'm stupid', and scratch at her arms causing bleeding and scabs. She suffered from bad dreams and imaginings relating to her past experiences. She was self-blaming at these times.

On the positive side, Elise demonstrated a mature use of language, very good vocabulary and she was able to express herself clearly and talk about her feelings. She had a good memory and was interested and enthusiastic about the world around her. She had a good sense of humour at times and was able to recite and understand jokes.

Making sense of behaviour

Fear of the unknown

It was apparent on one school visit that Elise was distracted and started fiddling anxiously when a new story was suggested. When asked 'Are you feeling worried?' she replied, 'Yes'. When asked, 'About the story?' she replied, 'I'm worried it might be scary.' It was reassuring for Elise to look at all the pictures and talk through the story before reading it.

Elise was persuaded to think about which lessons made her feel uncomfortable. Upon reflection, she realised that she did not like it when she did not know what was going to happen. Elise's teaching assistant reported that during a history session, she had become very restless and left the classroom for seemingly no reason. When asked what the topic had been, and on hearing herself say it was about child evacuees (children leaving their parents to go to live with unknown adults) she then realised that Elise's behaviour was understandable. For Elise, reassurance and advance warning of lesson content from the teaching assistant helped to reduce her anxiety levels and keep her in class.

> For some children who have experienced the loss of their birth parents and siblings, even the vocabulary used can at times be emotive. What do the words 'take away' (used in maths during a lesson on subtraction) trigger for a child who has suffered loss or been taken into care? For another Wellie Wednesday child, lessons on subtraction and division, i.e. 'splitting up' numbers, resulted in her disrupting the lesson, whilst lessons in addition and multiplication were not a problem.

Another child, Yan, refused to read and would not listen to stories read aloud. When asked, 'I wonder why you don't like new stories?' he replied, 'I don't know if scary things are going to happen.' When encouraged to look at all the pictures first, he was then able to settle down to listening to the story. The teaching assistant was advised to give a synopsis of any texts to be used and reassurance about the content of the story. She was also advised to give advance warning of lesson content in order to reduce anxiety levels.

When children have experienced life as being unpredictable, fearful and anxiety-raising, they come to school bringing with them a survival strategy of avoidance of the unknown. Learning is about entering into exploration of new information and the acquisition of skills through new experiences, so avoidance is not a successful learning strategy.

Soothing activities

Use of calming visualisation

In follow-up sessions, Elise was given one-to-one times of quiet with a member of the team. Initially, the Rainbow Garden visualisation (see Chapter 16) was too difficult. For Elise, the fear of intrusive thoughts brought panic, so at first silent time was spent together colouring in mandalas; allowing her to practise quiet concentration. The word mandala means circle and can be used as a means to quiet the mind as the centre becomes the focus of attention (www.free-mandala.com). Despite Elise finding art activities difficult, the reassuring mandala pattern, making colouring from outside-edge to ever-decreasing areas until the centre was reached, proved soothing for her.

For Elise, the circle was already a positive image as Wellie Wednesday used the concept of final circle time and the circle of friends candle holder. Later, whilst colouring, she could cope with hearing the visualisation read and finally she was able to enter into it.

The small glittery rainbow twin puppets were always greeted with affection by Elise, even as she struggled to enjoy their company in her imagination. Somehow, she knew she wanted to be able to relax into safe use of her imagination.

For children who have experienced difficult and traumatic events, using their imagination causes deep-seated fear, presumably of what thoughts might be unleashed. These children often struggle with artistic and creative activities. For them, plenty of playful experimentation with attractive materials helps them to gain enjoyment from creativity. Cutting, sticking, collage making, colourful abstract pattern making and printing activities may allow them to feel confident in using their imagination.

Some teachers have found that creating a box of soothing activities for a vulnerable child can then be used when there are signs of distress or anxiety. The contents will vary for each child, for example, a favourite book (often a non-fiction book full of illustrations and information), word searches or dot-to-dot puzzle activities, a gel or sand timer. Sometimes, something special given by a significant adult helps them to regain self-control, for example, for one child a lavender-filled pin cushion to hold and sniff had a calming effect.

Understanding comfortable and uncomfortable feelings

Children will develop their own emotional survival strategies, often uniquely inventive. They develop resilience in many ways. Elise, who had had very difficult things happen in her life, said that when she doesn't want to hear: 'I go deaf, completely deaf. I like going deaf when I don't want to hear.' Perhaps she knew best what she could and could not cope with hearing. To help children develop a better understanding of emotions we used many ways of expanding their vocabulary and recognition of their own and others' feelings. One important message was that 'everyone has feelings and that feelings can be comfortable or uncomfortable. In addition, all feelings need to be acknowledged but what we do with our feelings can be "OK or NOT OK".' For example, in the case of another child, he said: 'I feel like hitting [him] when [he] is being very annoying.' He was praised for knowing how he felt and for not using a 'NOT OK' behaviour (Greenberg and Kusche 1995).

Feelings Thermometer

On a follow-up visit to Elise in school, it was found that she was having a difficult time at home; she started talking then became increasingly distressed saying, 'I was born deaf ... I'm ugly, I'm ugly, I'm ugly', getting louder with every repetition. The response was to pass her the 'Feelings Thermometer' and say, 'You are having uncomfortable feelings?' She took it and put the peg right at the highest point on the scale. She then immediately started an activity. After a while she returned to the scale and moved the peg into the comfortable range. When asked what had helped her to get her feelings into being comfortable, she said: 'I turned uncomfortable into comfortable ... doing something else can help with uncomfortable feelings.'

Having taught children that feelings can be accepted even when they are uncomfortable, it is then important that adults do not try to persuade a child that they are not experiencing uncomfortable feelings. Had Elise been told, whilst she was in obvious distress, that she was not ugly or deaf, this would have been unlikely to be helpful to her. By remaining with her and supporting her in identifying what she was feeling, then allowing her a quiet time to soothe herself with a calming activity, she was able to come through it and gain insight from the experience.

Changes noticed in Elise

Elise did not forget what she had experienced. Some time after this when she said she was bored, discussion of being bored was not entered into, instead she was asked: 'How can you change bored?' Elise responded by getting on with the task, after a while she said: 'I turned bored into doing.' She was congratulated: 'You made a good choice to concentrate on "doing" and then your uncomfortable feelings changed.' 'Yes, to comfortable ones,' she replied, smiling.

> It has been shown that schools can act as a secure base for children who have experienced attachment difficulties (Geddes 2006). When regular routines and familiarity are coupled with kind, caring, consistent adults taking charge, children can often start to thrive as they find interest and success in learning. For looked-after children who attended Wellie Wednesday this was the case, as their schools did all they could to remain supportive and be familiar places for the children to return to each day, even as they experienced moves to new care placements. Schools who can offer caring consistency along with flexible support do much to assist vulnerable children to succeed, both academically and in developing the essential socio-emotional aspects of learning.

Elise's fragile sense of self seemed to gradually change. She was helped to feel better about herself through soothing activities and a growing understanding of thoughts, feelings and behaviour. Of her own accord, she found at times, when she acknowledged her uncomfortable feelings, she could even change them to comfortable ones.

Reflection

When behaviour 'comes out of nowhere', could it be anxiety-driven? How can an awareness of triggers be more fully understood to support the child?

References

Geddes, H. (2006). *Attachment in the classroom: The links between children's early experience, emotional wellbeing and performance in school*. London: Worth Publishing.

Greenberg, M. and Kusche, C. (1995). *Promoting alternative thinking strategies (PATHS)*. South Deerfield: Channing-Bete.

Chapter 12

Self-hatred and self-harming
What is special about Kevin and Anna?

Everybody deserves kindness.
People who have a lot of kindness have some to give away.

(Anna)

Kevin and Anna were two children who attended the pupil referral unit for small group work. Although they did not attend the Wellie Wednesday project, similar strategies were used to help them. They have been included in this book because poor self-image is common for many vulnerable children and addressing their attitudes towards themselves is fundamental to them making progress socially and in their learning. Anna and Kevin represent this specific type of difficulty and the approaches used to enable change.

In Paul Gilbert's book *The Compassionate Mind* (2009), he describes studies demonstrating that developing kindness and compassion for self and others can help in calming down the threat system: as a mother's care and love soothes a baby's distress, so we can learn to calm our own distressing emotions and actually increase feelings of contentment and well-being. It is always distressing when children feel they are unlovable. Expressions of self-hatred and self-harming behaviour are ideally the province of experienced Child and Adolescent Mental Health Service (CAMHS) doctors and therapists. However, waiting lists are long and in the meantime, schools are faced with the challenge of how to respond to such distressing behaviour.

Receiving kindness, gentleness, warmth and compassion help induce feeling soothed and settled, levels of the stress hormones reduce, a sense of security is stimulated reducing the negative emotions.

(Gilbert 2009)

Pen picture of Kevin

Kevin was referred for help by his school, who were particularly concerned about his escalating self-hatred. His frequent outbursts of 'I hate myself' and 'I am going to kill myself' were distressing for all. His teachers and teaching assistant had tried to respond with 'We like you' or 'It upsets us when you say that' or 'We would be very sad if you did that' but the more they tried to persuade him not to feel self-hatred, the more and louder he repeated himself.

Such emotive words also served as an instant way to achieve adult attention. But rather than seeing this behaviour as 'attention seeking', it may be more helpful and compassionate to see these children as 'attention needing', then it is easier to look for the cause of their behaviour, for example, lack of independence, learning difficulty, emotional insecurity, anxiety.

Developing a positive sense of self

Establishing core beliefs and an awareness of the brain

Kevin was introduced to Wellie Wednesday's core beliefs, but with the addition of being kind to ourselves as well as others, because of the nature of the severity of his and Anna's negativity towards themselves. 'We follow instructions' was omitted as there were safeguarding issues relating to these children. Indiscriminate following of instructions could endanger the safety of vulnerable children in some circumstances.

> We are kind to ourselves and to each other.
> We keep ourselves and each other safe.
> We look after the environment.

The response that was given to any child's outburst of self-hatred was, 'Is that being kind to yourself?', then a reminder, 'Remember we are kind to ourselves and each other and we keep ourselves safe. Is that safe behaviour if you end up being hurt?'

The children also became familiar with the model of the brain and were taught that kindness given and received have a beneficial effect on the brain and its healthy development.

These concepts were explicitly taught through acts of kindness being pointed out and references were made to how others felt when someone was kind. Safety was also referred to, especially when a child was behaving recklessly: 'We need to keep you safe' or 'We care about you and need to keep you safe.' Such statements at times of heightened emotion served to remind the child we were there to care and support not to reject or be punitive. These de-escalating reminders were usually effective.

It can never be assumed that kindness is understood as not all children have experienced kindness as a normal part of their lives. Kevin's times of anger, frustration, refusal and anxiety initially elicited tirades of self-hatred. He was gently reminded 'We are kind to ourselves', then 'Is that being kind to yourself?'

Building relationships

Adults did not respond by mirroring Kevin's disquiet but by allowing him time to assimilate the need for self-compassion and for him to sense their supportive calm drawing him back to the group. It seemed that the more Kevin learnt about kindness the more of it he wanted. He started to come alongside or lean against the adults saying 'I like you, you are kind.' He was not alone, children it seems are hyper-alert to experiences of kindness and soon start to enjoy 'paying it forward' by 'committing daily acts of random kindness' (see Pay it Forward, Catherine Ryan Hyde, 2010).

Heartmath (www.heartmath.com/institute-of-heartmath/) research shows that the heart's energy fields become incoherent when experiencing stress, anger, distress or anxiety. Those nearby will be affected and they too will either experience incoherent rhythms themselves or their coherent rhythm can bring the other back to coherence more quickly. Therefore, when one child was exhibiting disruptive behaviour, it was important for the adults to remain calm and bring the group back to a coherent energy rhythm. Otherwise it is all too easy for disruption to spread at times when one child becomes agitated, angry or aggressive.

Good ignoring

In order to prevent the spread of disruption when a child experienced overwhelming feelings, the children learnt that one of our targets was 'good ignoring', taught to them by the puppet called Iggy Ignore (see Chapter 1). Reminders were given for good ignoring as soon as another child became disruptive. By keeping the group focused, the calming effect would enable the off task child to rejoin the group as quickly as possible. Initial ignoring is used, prefaced by 'I can see you are feeling upset at the moment, take some time out to feel calm again. When you feel better come back and join us.' Then the child is given time to move away, calm down and return. If this does not occur then the child is not left to escalate disruptive and even dangerous behaviour. In these cases, in order to remove an audience the child would still be encouraged to move away and spend more time in their 'safe place' whilst reminded in a calm and friendly voice, 'Come back when you are ready to join in.' A teaching assistant would monitor from a distance, avoiding eye contact or conversation but quietly reassures with, 'I'm here to help when you are ready.' The teacher's emphasis needs to remain on giving positive attention to the on task group. As soon as possible after the child returns to the group, quiet words of praise were given: 'Well done for getting on with your work', 'That is good sitting', 'Good listening Kevin' or 'Good waiting. It will be your turn to read soon.' The child quickly gains positive attention for what they are now doing right, thereby reassuring them that their behaviour has not caused them to be rejected. This is not the time to explore the previous behaviour; that needs to wait until connection has been re-established, ideally some success achieved and the child feels secure that they still belong. The fragile emotional state of vulnerable children, especially those who have experienced rejection, requires that the first need when dysregulated behaviour escalates, is to have their uncomfortable feelings contained. Hearing that others are remaining calm and the adults are maintaining safety helps the child to cope.

When a child was behaving defiantly or dangerously, the procedure then was to remove the other children quickly and calmly whilst the teacher stayed with the distressed child and facilitated de-escalation and calming. A delicate balance was kept between focusing on praising positive behaviour and ensuring a vulnerable child at no point was made to feel forgotten or rejected whilst preventing the negative behaviour from gaining maximum attention.

The period after an outburst, is a crucial time, seen as a window of opportunity for building connection and trust. The child who has experienced extreme feelings and out of control behaviour is usually in a vulnerable state and in need of reassurance and soothing. If, at this time, the adults involved can be emotionally available, then frequently the child will accept comfort and support. When this occurs a further step of trust in the reliability of the adult is built, enabling the child to believe they are there to care, support and help them. Next time the feelings are difficult to contain, the reassuring words and clear direction of the adult are more likely to successfully bring about de-escalation sooner.

Changes noticed in Kevin

One of the ways the transfer of regulation of emotion from parents or carers to their young children occurs is through the acquisition of language. As a child learns to express their emotions in words, they have less need for angry outbursts or crying to indicate how they are feeling. Using feelings language as much as possible helped the children to hear adults modelling responses to their own feelings. Where previously they might only have known happy, sad, angry and excited, hearing how others expressed their emotions allowed them to learn additional words to express their own feelings. As Kevin learnt a new vocabulary of feelings he no longer needed to resort to self-hatred every time he felt frustrated, cross or anxious. Instead, he began to separate not being able to do something, i.e. mastery of a skill, from his own fragile identity. His self-image gradually began to reshape as he experienced success, for example, 'I like reading', 'I am good at puzzles', 'I can help you'.

Soon he became able to join compliments time. At first he would give genuine thoughtful compliments to others but when it was his turn to receive a compliment he would interrupt or leave the group. Anything good did not seem to fit his perceived self-image and therefore perhaps he felt it could not be for him or that he did not deserve it. It was not considered that it would be helpful to him if we tried to persuade or cajole him to accept compliments that he couldn't believe in. This needed to wait until he could identify himself with experiences of success. Gradually, as he accumulated new positive social, emotional and learning experiences, and with a file full of completed work, he began to feel worthy of hearing compliments about himself. Setting up the compliments time circle soon became a sought after treasured time for him. He put so much tenderness into arranging the circle to be special for everyone. At Christmas, the addition of a Nativity scene lit by candles and his contented face glowing in the candlelight was deeply moving, a reminder to us of how kindness had changed a troubled heart and mind.

A positive self-image is created through experiences that show self-worth. Self-esteem programmes generally want to draw on past positive experiences and for fragile and vulnerable children these can prove unsuitable. What is transformative is exposure to opportunities to succeed, for example, to be responsible, to help another, to be trusted, to persevere, to instigate and reciprocate laughter and playfulness. These are the kind of experiences that develop a sense of self-worth.

Pen picture of Anna

Anna had had a difficult history and had been moved from one school to another. Her challenging behaviour included defiance, refusal to cooperate, running out of school and hurting other children. She would tease and say unkind things to her peers and her frequent lying caused staff to distrust her. Her learning was affected by her poor concentration and lack of interest in attempting work. The result of this persistent behaviour was that she was excluded from school. At home she was independent and was at risk due to her enjoyment of wandering away from home, visiting local shops and hanging around with older children.

Developing a positive sense of self

Acknowledging self

A poster on the classroom wall of a bulldog with a little kitten between its paws and a caption saying 'To have a friend you need to be a friend' was used with saying our shared belief 'We are kind to ourselves and each other'. Anna commented: 'I'm not even a friend to myself, I pull my own hair out.' This moment of self-revelation then enabled her to start to make changes. Anna was encouraged to write a reminder to herself. On a post-it note she wrote 'I will be kind to myself' and stuck it to the group poster.

Avoiding self-blame

Through expanding her vocabulary of feelings, Anna came to understand that she was not to blame for her feelings. Picture cards of bears were used that showed different expressions and body language (The Bears: www.inventiveplus.co.uk). These encouraged discussion and empathic understanding. In order for Anna to understand how other people felt, she first needed to accurately acknowledge her own feelings. The picture cards gave her the opportunity to imagine the circumstances that might have resulted in these images, for example, the bear looks sad because he is feeling left out by his friends.

Developing empathy

A set of scenario cards was created describing various situations. Anna took her turn to choose a card, step onto a pair of footprints and talk about what might happen next to the person described. For example, 'Tommy took his sister's pencil case to school and lost some of the felt tip pens. How did Tommy feel? What happened next?' Through experiencing 'being in someone else's shoes', Anna was able to explore possible different responses and their effects without feeling blame or personal responsibility.

Changes noticed in Anna

In the following weeks and months Anna became increasingly gentle and thoughtful in her actions. She was extremely perceptive when giving compliments, noticing others' achievements and showing a new generosity of spirit. At the end of term, when asked if she still needed the post-it as a reminder, she said, 'I haven't pulled my hair out for ages.' When asked what had changed for her, she said, 'I am kind now.'

On her last day when she was presented with the dog and kitten poster, her face lit up with delight. Not only did she love the picture but it held for her a much more significant meaning. For her, it had acted as the key that unlocked her true potential as a kind and caring person. When talking about starting at a new school and being asked what would be different this time, she replied she would be kind at her new school now that she knew it was important.

As Kevin and Anna learnt to be kind about (and to) themselves, so it followed that they were able to be kind to others. As they observed:

> Everyone can be kind if they think to be kind.
>
> (Kevin)

> Everybody deserves kindness. People who have a lot of kindness have some to give away.
>
> (Anna)

Reflection

How can we recognise those children who need help learning to be kind about and to themselves?

References

Gilbert, P. (2009). *The compassionate mind*. London: Constable & Robinson Ltd.
Ryan, Hyde, C. (2010). Pay It Forward. New York: Simon and Schuster.
The Bears. www.inventiveplus.co.uk. Northampton: Inventive Plus.

Chapter 13

The competitive spirit
What is special about Seth?

I will definitely remember Liam and Shaun, they are my friends.
I liked Richard saving the sheep, he is my super hero, he thought about the sheep and not about his shoes getting wet.

(Seth)

Pen picture of Seth

Seth was an extremely competitive child who demonstrated negativity, disregard and put-downs towards other children. He found it difficult to accept constraints and to accommodate to others. He was often distracted and had difficulty in making constructive responses. Seth also presented as an anxious child who had an insecure sense of self. It was felt that he was not reaching his potential.

Seth was energetic and enthusiastic, capable and driven. He was able to connect experiences and was capable of constructive participation. A competitive spirit has fired many people to great achievements. Sport relies on its participants having a desire to win. However, for some children, the competitive spirit stems from rivalry for time and positive attention and a struggle to live with comparison. Seth was driven by his need to 'win'. He made everything a competition from 'I'll race you' to 'I can eat faster than you' and 'I'll be first in line'. He had little understanding of cooperation or how others might feel when he used put-downs and disparaging comments: 'Your painting is rubbish', 'My lunch box is newer than yours', the scope seemed endless. Sadly, these predominating attitudes meant Seth lacked good friends.

Evidence from evolutionary biology indicates that whilst the biological systems required for competition are active, the caring soothing system is inactive. Only one of these neuronal systems can fire at any one time (Porges 2007). When young children feel constantly driven to strive to be best, biggest, strongest, fastest, this will inevitably raise issues of comparison, and with possible achievement there will also be experiences of sensing inferiority and failure. Coping with these mixed emotions requires a degree of emotional security, of knowing that losing does not detract from a sense of personal self-worth.

When a child's soothing system has had insufficient development (through lack of warmth, connectedness and acceptance), they may well struggle to feel safe and calm or to show empathy and caring behaviour towards others. Sometimes, children with a poorly developed sense of self try to compensate by proving themselves competitively. However, when this is combined with an inability to manage their feelings, social interactions can become destructive, with frequent outbursts or sulking, and may lead to further feelings of alienation or isolation. Signs of an over-competitive attitude with poor social skills may indicate that a child is suffering from feelings of low self-worth. In Seth's case this was backed up by his Boxall profile (Bennathan and Boxall 1998).

It was felt that Seth needed to learn to accept constraints and develop his cooperative skills. It was hoped that he would develop kind and helpful behaviour and see himself as a good friend, accommodating to others. One of the main aims was to support Seth in reaching a greater understanding of being able to take part but to learn to keep winning in perspective. Most importantly the aim was for Seth to build a positive sense of self-worth.

Building self-worth

Developing empathy

For Seth, rather than trying to quash his competitiveness, which led to him experiencing some positive feelings of satisfaction and self-worth, the focus was on giving him the experiences that would further develop his soothing, contentment and connectedness system. In order for Seth to develop empathy he needed to feel the benefits of our group commitment:

> We are kind to each other.
> We keep ourselves and each other safe.

In Seth's case, he needed to experience more of the emotional safety that would allow him to feel calmer, more contented and better engaged in warm social interactions. These experiences would increase the activation of his para sympathetic nervous system.

Building trust

A primary target for Seth was to learn to gain pleasure from working with his step-father and peers at activities that did not involve winners and losers. One of the first activities was a blindfold game to build trust. It involved an obstacle course to be negotiated by children and adults working in pairs but one was blindfolded and needed to be led by the other. Seth had no consideration for his 'blind' partner. Initially, he could only focus on finishing the course before the other pairs with little concern for his (long suffering!) partner's well-being. Despite explanation and instructions, as soon as he started he would race to the end of the course triumphant that everyone else was still slowly working their way towards the finishing line. It was pointed out that his partner stood stationary awaiting the necessary guidance to complete the course.

Finally, he understood that his role was not to run his fastest because it was not a race, but a challenge to keep his partner safe by leading him carefully through the obstacle course because he was unable to see the things that were in their way. Seth changed his aim from winning by himself, to successfully completing the course with his partner without bumping into any of the obstacles. Once grasped, he enjoyed the responsibility and as we cleared up he said: 'I wish my mum was here to do that with.'

Great minds think alike: accommodating to others

Seth was competitive to the point of outrage on hearing 'his' answer spoken by a peer who had been asked to answer a question. Seth was not alone in resenting others getting things right when they had also thought of the correct answer (see Ashley Chapter 5). To help them come to terms with this the concept of 'great minds think alike' was introduced with a sign of touching their head and giving a thumbs up to each other. This established it as a positive connection with the thinking of others. When Seth guessed what we were going to do next, with a piece of equipment or when he thought correctly that it was time for lunch 'Well done Seth, that is "great minds think alike", he was told.'

When he suggested leaving something behind on the last day, he was delighted when he saw bird seed being handed around to scatter and leave for the birds to find. This time, knowing his idea had already been thought of elicited a huge smile and the chant, 'Great minds think alike!'

Changes noticed in Seth

As time went on, Seth derived more pleasure from cooperative activities; we saw a softer side emerging and smiles replaced his former tense expression. He understood the pleasure of sharing instead of trying to grab everything for himself. He demonstrated his new-found trust in the adults when he was heard whispering to another child, 'We are each going to get some.' He also started to notice other people's actions and reflected on their motives. After watching Richard rescue a lamb found in a stream, Seth said: 'I liked Richard saving the sheep, he is my hero. Richard thought about the sheep and not about getting his shoes wet.' This was later used in a narrative approach to problem-solving session with Seth. He was asked what might help him to get things right in school. He replied: 'I could think about Richard in my imagination when I am stuck (like the lamb was stuck). I could think about him being invisible but I could be happy because he would help me and no-one knows.'

Soon after the lamb-saving incident, Seth and Liam were running from their tents and he was deliberately keeping pace beside the much less athletic Liam. As they arrived, laughing together, he said: 'Normally I run and be first but Liam and I were first together. Maybe we can do it again.' It was a moment of great delight to see that Seth had chosen to ignore his desire to be first in favour of the pleasures of having fun with a friend. He now understood that not everything needed to be made into a competition because sometimes good times are to be had that are not about winning.

Seth had experienced the benefits of playfulness, fun and friendship without the constant need for winners and losers. In addition, he was now able to enjoy sporting competition more fully, having swapped unkind behaviour for teamwork and sportsmanship.

Reflection

Consider the need to progress from the negative aspects of the competitive spirit (for example, belittling the attempts of others, seeing all activities as a competition), to the positive aspects of the competitive spirit (for example, teamwork, fair play and encouraging the efforts of others).

References

Bennathan, M. and Boxall, M. (1998). *The Boxall profile: A guide to effective intervention in the education of pupils with Emotional and Behavioural Difficulties; Handbook for teachers.* Nurture Group Consortium; Association of Workers for Children with Emotional and Behavioural Difficulties. Maidstone: AWCEBD.

Porges, S.W. (2007). *The polyvagal theory: Neurophysical foundations of emotions, attachment communications and self regulation.* New York: W.W. Norton and Company.

Chapter 14

Building independence and responsibility

What is special about Liam?

I don't want to do this but I'll do it anyway.

(Liam)

Pen picture of Liam

Liam had difficulty in sitting still. At listening times he was very restless, jumpy and was distracted by his own ideas and thoughts. He had trouble following more complex instructions involving several steps. He was impulsive. He had become used to being helped as soon as any difficulty, however small, arose. He was secure in the knowledge that his mother was ever-ready to offer a helping hand, as she thought he would benefit from her ideas to achieve what she saw as a 'better' result.

At times the group was involved in problem-solving investigations, requiring reflective thinking in order to come to a range of possible outcomes. These would then be discussed in order to find a final solution. It was less about coming up with the right answer and more about developing the thought processes involved in problem-solving. Liam's helpful mother was anxious to enable him to give the 'correct answer'. With every good intention she would whisper the answer in his ear or take over the task herself, thus depriving him of the opportunity to develop his thinking and to make his own choices.

Liam had a deeply enquiring mind. He demonstrated an imaginative use of language and a good sense of humour. He wanted to get on with people and enjoyed cooperation and sharing. He showed creative flair.

As children grow, it is a natural stage of development for them to strive for independence. Without it, the baby would not want to explore beyond its parent's arms. Watching toddlers trying to pull themselves up to stand and struggling to clamber onto a chair are early examples of the child making independent decisions and developing new skills. Children should have a natural desire to explore and as they grow older they need to continue this as a journey towards independence and ultimately a successful transition into the adult world. Inevitably, the developmental challenges and risks become greater. Learning to assess risk in order to keep oneself safe can only be achieved through 'doing', albeit with varying degrees of encouragement, support and guidance.

Learning to be independent and take responsibility

Encouraging independent achievement

Children need to learn how to work things out for themselves instead of expecting adults to step in. Liam was used to his mother always being nearby, watching for signs of indecision. Some adults find it difficult to allow children to create things in ways that to them do not seem the best way; they feel a need to rescue the situation when they see a child struggling. They often feel the need to ensure that the child gets it right, focusing on the result rather than the process involved.

At Wellie Wednesday, children were frequently offered activities where 'learning through doing' was the primary purpose. Sometimes, there may not have been an end product; the purpose had been to learn from the process. It is important to understand that learning to persevere and to feel proud of independent achievement is an important part of children reaching a realistic sense of self as an individual. The opportunity for Liam to work with a range of adults, who offered encouragement but did not take over the task, gave him an experience that delighted him. He would say: 'I did this by myself.'

Parents and carers were often surprised by what their children could achieve. It usually started at breakfast on the first day, when for some children pouring their own cereal and milk was a new experience. Liam refused, saying: 'I'm not allowed to, I'll spill it'. Our response was: 'It's OK. We will teach you how to do it so it doesn't spill.' By using small quantities in a jug and the advice 'slowly and carefully' whilst standing by to ensure success, Liam was off to a good start and his mother was impressed and proud of him.

Persisting through difficulty

We saw a change in Liam as he started to work with persistence and a determination to succeed. One task was to use a rope to drag back two pieces of wood that were too big to carry. The children were thrilled with their pieces of rope but, for some, how to attach them to pieces of wood was a mystery. Dangling the rope above the wood, one child obviously assumed it would miraculously tie itself around the logs. Very few children had experience of tying knots.

Liam failed several times to secure his chosen log, then he spied an old drawer on a pile of firewood and decided this would be an easier option, so he pulled it off and eventually managed to tie the rope around it. Dragging it back through mud and up slopes had him straining every muscle as he slipped in the mud, which had previously been a problem, but now he began to delight in the messiness of the whole experience. He was supported with words of encouragement: 'It doesn't matter how long it takes, keep going and you'll get there in the end.' The others finished, with their smaller pieces of branches, and they returned to cheer Liam on. When he finally reached the fireside he had bonded with his drawer and wanted to take it to his tent. We were delighted to have seen Liam laughing, his usual serious expression replaced with smiles.

Perseverance was now a concept he understood. He was asked: 'When might persevering be helpful in school Liam?' He was able to think of maths when any mistake would make him cross but now he thought he could have another go. At good news time the next week he said: 'I got something wrong, I didn't complain but I thought I'll do this again right.'

Changes noticed in Liam

Liam's mother had not thought about allowing him to spread his own toast or pour his drink. Previously, she had thought that doing everything for her children was what she was meant to do to 'be a good mummy'. But when she saw how much he could do, she recognised his need to master these sorts of skills.

Parents and carers were often surprised to find that being given responsibilities was very different in outcome to being given chores as a punishment. Responsibilities in school are sought after and highly regarded, for example, library or register monitors. At Wellie Wednesday, the children were praised for helping with jobs, for example, the washing up, collecting firewood, peeling, grating and cutting up vegetables, pouring drinks, collecting water. They were encouraged to show their parent or carer how responsible they could be. In return, the children felt trusted and experienced a sense of pride.

Liam was also given more responsibility at home and the praise to go with it, for example, pouring the cereal and milk at breakfast, having a box containing scissors, glue and small items to be used at the table away from his younger sibling. Previously, his mother had only managed to cope with both children by denying Liam age-appropriate toys and activities because of their potential danger to the younger child.

His mother's good news after a few weeks was that at the weekend she and Liam's father had listened from upstairs as Liam got breakfast for his sister. They heard cupboard and fridge open and both children talking happily. She resisted worrying about how he had reached the cereal bowls. When they left the kitchen to play elsewhere she went down to see what she would find. No mess, no spills, the cereal and milk put away and the washing up in the sink. Liam had solved the problem of the bowls by using two plastic boxes obtainable from a low cupboard! Mum and Dad were impressed and pleased that this joint activity had also resulted in the siblings getting on really well together.

With more responsibility, Liam's independence increased and his previously learnt helplessness diminished. His frustration with wanting to do things himself, then giving up and letting his mother take over, was reduced as she learnt to stand back but offer words of encouragement and believe in his abilities. For example, when he was doing model-making she said: 'Give yourself thinking time and I'm sure you will work out a way to stick it together.'

Liam's own comments showed insight into his greater understanding and the impact this had had on how he had changed: '"Trouble" all my lifetime makes me get upset. I'm trying not to give him attention. He turned into major trouble. Now I'm trying to help him shrink and be good and turn into "Goody"' (see Chapter 19).

Chapter 15

Food

Too much? Too little? Fussy eater? Fearful?

I will always remember John's marvellous menus.

(Elise)

Food is a primary need and the giving and sharing of food is a vital way of nurturing. Mealtimes provided opportunities for learning healthy eating habits, experimenting with new tastes, developing good manners and enjoying each other's company. The atmosphere around the fire at mealtimes was joyful, relaxed and socially enriching. Parents, carers and children enjoyed making mealtimes a much broader experience and not just focused on what was and was not being eaten.

A range of habitual behaviour around food was noticed. These were causing concern and tension at home:

- Emma and Amber used delaying tactics, for example, whining and complaining voices to spin out mealtimes. This ensured that their parents were unable to turn their attention to anything else whilst the children toyed with their food.
- Yasmin used crying to weaken her parents' resolve. She had reached the point where fear of her tears meant that her food demands were complied with: she was only eating a diet limited to her favourite foods.
- At home, Ned chose not to eat what was on offer, saying 'I am not hungry', preferring to wait for tasty snacks (crisps and biscuits) that would be provided when he later complained that he was hungry.
- At other times Ned was unable to regulate the amount of food he could eat, taking large amounts that he then could not finish.
- For Dillon and Yan, much more serious reasons were underlying their difficulties around eating. This was evident from the tension, the pallour and subsequent vomiting. In both cases it was recognised that there was genuine fear and high levels of anxiety and not mere fussiness.
- For Yan, the idea of different foods touching each other on one plate caused distress.
- One mother's expectation that her child would not eat what was on offer indicated to him how she expected him to behave. When the expectations changed he began to experiment with new foods.

- Elise, Ashley and Ellie communicated deep-rooted fears about whether there would be enough food for them as well as everyone else. This was demonstrated by:
  - asking repeatedly when it would be lunch or snack time
  - wanting to take far more than they could eat
  - saying 'I'm hungry' at regular intervals.
- Elise and Zak regularly tried to eat non-food items, such as pencils, rubbers, Blu-Tack, paper clips and paper.

Gaining attention from adults

Children quickly learn that their parents and carers respond with attention if they complain, protest, show distress or refuse to eat what is offered. In the same way as any other behaviour, it will be repeated if attention is earned by it.

Adults felt upset when they had spent time preparing a meal that was then refused. From birth, food and feeding can cause anxiety for parents and carers; they were quick to acknowledge that it is a very emotive area for them, which can cause frustration and concerns. This often resulted in adults avoiding upset by only presenting their child with food they knew they would like.

A limited acceptance of different tastes

Developing the sense of taste is not necessarily a pleasant experience. For many children, even trying a new food for the first time is refused in case it is unpleasant. For others, one disliked taste experience will never be repeated. It may help to realise that children's aversion to new tastes is a natural response. It is a safety strategy developed in our evolutionary past. In the days of our ancestors there would have been a real threat of poisoning. Taking time to develop a new taste for new foods by trying small quantities first of all was a protective strategy.

It is known that in order to familiarise our taste buds with a new taste, at least ten (Eartmans, A., *et al* 2001, Birch, L., 1998) experiences are required, so a reasonable strategy is to expect children to taste a new food realising that it will take them a few tries to become accustomed to the taste.

Establishing positive thoughts and behaviour relating to food

Our lunchtime meal was for adults and children to share, everyone ate the same food together. This allowed for modelling of how to deal with eating unfamiliar foods. Everyone was served their meal and if something was on the menu they did not like they were encouraged to say 'This is not my favourite thing' and to accept a tiny amount on their plate. It was explained to them that the cooks had worked hard all morning to make the lunch so to refuse it would make them feel unhappy. They learnt that saying 'yuck' or 'that's horrible' was unacceptable as it was unkind. They also learnt that they did not always have to speak their thoughts. Frequently, children tend to say what they think automatically. Learning not to make unkind comments is an important part of developing empathy.

They learnt that:

- Different types of food are required for our bodies to grow and be healthy.
- Water is good for the body, particularly the brain: 'brain juice'.
- Our taste buds enjoy some tastes more than others.
- Some people's favourite food is someone else's least favourite.
- Disliking a taste can prevent us from eating what our bodies need.
- Disliking a taste does not mean that the food is going to harm you.

Changing the language seemed to have a remarkably freeing effect on the children's previously entrenched behaviour. 'It's not my favourite thing' was taken up by Emma and her mother to great effect. Mealtimes stopped being a source of aggravation to Emma's mother as she found that she no longer needed to cajole and entice her. Instead, Emma joined mealtimes happily.

For Dillon, his nausea around food was gradually diminished and his anxiety levels reduced as he learnt to use self-calming strategies.

Ed had never eaten potatoes except in the form of chips. By involving him in the preparation of mashed potato, he became interested in trying something new.

Yan's dislike of foods touching each other was addressed initially by using a plate with several compartments. He was able to accept foods being on his plate even if he struggled with eating them. The mixed fruit was soon accepted served on one ordinary plate having been introduced on the plate with separate sections.

Many children were not used to drinking water. After learning about the benefits of water, they were involved in using water carriers to collect drinking water. Each person was given a labelled cup that was available to them at any time. Children enjoyed taking it in turns to pour from a jug.

For those who had concerns about getting enough food, they were reassured by the cook, stating 'There is enough for everyone' as preparations for serving began. Children were encouraged to have a small first helping but more would be available if they wanted it. This avoided the need to try to take as much as possible, over-estimating how much they could eat. They came to realise that second helpings would be available.

Eating together and sharing the same meal was an important way to enhance feelings of group identity. In his first week, Neil was delighted to see that he and Annabelle, who he was sitting next to, had the same food. For some children who were used to a packed lunch, and families eating individual meals at home, this was a new experience: 'Look I have got two sausages, cheesy mashed potato, baked beans on my plate and you have got two sausages, cheesy mashed potato and baked beans on yours!'

Other benefits of the shared meal were:

- Watching food prepared and cooked in the outdoors.
- Creating a recipe book, *John's Marvellous Menus*, to which all contributed comments and ideas. This was compiled by a member of the team and all those taking part received a copy of the book to take home.
- Involving children, parents and carers in food preparation and helping to serve it, especially passing round a shared plate of fruit at snack time.

- Talking about other things at mealtimes; general conversation rather than focusing on food so that children did not feel that their eating was being watched.
- Communal enjoyment of food and all tasting a little of everything.
- A male role model planning the menu, food items, shopping and cooking on the open fire, demonstrating skills, interest and enjoyment.
- Adults modelling trying new tastes: 'It's not my favourite thing but I will have a little.'
- Use of mealtimes as an opportunity to enjoy conversations with the children. For one group, it became a weekly joke-telling session. At breakfast, good news was always shared.
- Understanding that chores can be enjoyable, for example, Neil moved from saying 'I'm not a servant', to taking on the responsibility of washing up and enjoying the fun of the water and washing up bubbles. From there, he first realised that he could gain pleasure from being kind and helpful.
- Messages about enjoyment of food were incorporated into songs.
- Having fun with food, for example, smiley faces with segments of oranges, making kebabs, toasting marshmallows on the fire.
- Helping to build the fire ready for cooking, which involved collecting wood, bringing it back to the cooking area and, under supervision, adding the wood to the fire.
- Planning food for the following week together but with additional new taste and novelty experiences being incorporated each week, for example, using a pineapple corer and peeler to excite interest in trying a new food.

Food and mealtimes played a central part in the nurturing atmosphere of the day: taste, smells and visual pleasure. The physical warmth of the fire encouraged everyone to feel the emotional warmth of the social gathering. Comments made included:

> I thought I didn't like fish cakes but once I tasted 'John's Fabulous Fish Cakes' I had two.

> Many of us were reluctant to try parsnip chips due to a strong dislike of parsnip. All of us were converted. They were amazing! Sweet and crispy. It just goes to show, you don't know until you try.

> I never had corn on the cob before. I buy it now!

> The mango was yummy, very juicy and sweet.

> I eat swede now!

Reflection

Consider the impact that food issues can have on children's social, emotional and physical well-being: Too much? Too little? Fussy eater? Fearful about food? Enjoyment of sharing food is central to social connection with a wider community. How can parents, carers and staff in school ensure an enjoyable approach to eating a wide variety of foods?

Chapter 16

A summary of strategies

A pathway to each child's successful future

The more we are together
Together, together
The more we are together
The happier we'll be
'Cause your friends are my friends
And my friends are your friends
The more we are together
The happier we'll be.

(Traditional folk song)

Developing positive interaction and establishing group cohesion

A number of strategies were used to help members of the group connect with each other. The aim was to ensure that everyone felt valued and to recognise that they each had a positive contribution to make to the group. This included the use of specific praise and compliments. In addition, everyone was encouraged to be aware not only of their own safety but also the safety of others.

Developing interaction through singing together

From the outset of the Wellie Wednesday project, singing played a significant part in establishing and building a sense of fun and togetherness. Words were written to the tunes of familiar songs and nursery rhymes so that most of the group would be familiar with the tunes. The songs incorporated elements of their day, for example, the song 'Wellie Wellie Wednesday is good fun' (to the tune of 'Twinkle Twinkle Little Star') talked about the enjoyment of the group sitting round the fire having been chosen to join the project.

Songs were sung on the minibus journey in the morning and on the way back to school at the end of the day. The welcome song 'The more we are together, the happier we'll be' named all members of the group and was sung at the beginning of each session. Including the names within the song allowed everyone a chance to very quickly learn each other's names. One child introduced the idea of being able to name everyone in the group and this then became a challenge for others to have a go!

At the end of the day the group sang together again 'Goodbye (naming each person in turn) we're glad you came today'. This reinforced the learning of everyone's names and acknowledged that we had been pleased to be together again. The farewell song also made a recognisable end to the day before leaving the final circle to depart on the minibus. Endings can be difficult times for some children and having a clearly defined routine was reassuring in its predictability. This needed to be brief about parting, positive about the week ahead in school and excited looking forward to the next meeting.

If someone was unable to attend due to illness, a message was written to say we were sorry they could not come and that they had been missed. This was given to the person at compliments time on their return the following week.

Singing together provided a way of communicating group expectations that had been identified on the target chart, for example, 'We are going to Wellie Wednesday' (to the tune of 'Glory Glory Alleluia') included phrases about good waiting, good sitting, good listening, good sharing, good thinking, good caring and about helping each other to 'get it right'.

The song 'What shall we do on Wellie Wednesday?' (to the tune of 'What shall we do with the Drunken Sailor?') celebrated the group identity and the activities that had taken place, for example, 'make a fire and eat our breakfast', 'walk in the woods and climb a tree'. The children helped to write the song, making suggestions of various activities that could be included.

One child on their first week had run off to show defiance and seemed to be testing our responses. Without chasing him he was brought back into the group by everyone using a call and response game. The following week a song was written, adapted from a traditional scout song, to stress the importance of knowing where everyone was and keeping them safe:

> Campfire's burning, campfire's burning
> Come nearer, come nearer,
> Where's Neil? Where's Neil? (naming each child)
> Let's sing and be merry.

As the project progressed, other songs were written to positively reinforce reminders about expectations.

- 'Our Beliefs' song (about being kind, keeping each other safe and looking after the environment) was sung at the beginning of each session.
- 'Wait and See' was about trusting and finding out later what was going to happen.
- 'Just a minute, let me think' reminded children to take time to think before speaking or doing something.
- 'The Voices' song was about using different voices in varying situations, especially the silent 'thinking voice'.

Non-verbal communication

Engaging adults in dialogue is a common way for a child to ensure that attention is focused upon them. Responses tend to elicit further comment and so it was useful at times to be able to use non-verbal signs as reminders that did not interrupt the flow of what was happening. Examples of non-verbal communication used and understood by all the group were:

- Three middle fingers held up meant 'wait and see'.
- Holding the target chart and a pen encouraged children to try hard without needing to say anything.
- The 'great minds think alike' signal, touching the head then thumbs up to the other person, encouraged children to celebrate having the same ideas as others.
- The 'rewind' signal, making a backward circular motion with the forefinger of one hand, meant that children could try again without worrying that they had made a mistake.
- Pointing to a blank speech bubble made of laminated card meant it was someone else's turn to speak.

These became unspoken agreements within the group.

Percussion instruments

Instruments were used by each child to create a band, building a sense of belonging. As they played their instruments the group formed a long line. They spiralled inwards and outwards playing their instruments, moving close and connecting with each other. The drumming, which became rhythmic whilst moving together and apart, had a calming and almost trance-like effect as it progressed.

Shared drawing and music making

A flip chart was set up using a large piece of paper and instruments were made available. One member of the group chose an instrument and began playing it with a regular beat. They then went to the chart and drew the first part of an imaginary woodland creature. Next, they chose someone else to join in, then returned to playing their own instrument. The second person chose an instrument and began playing, then went to the board and drew the next part of the creature, they then chose the third person to continue the drawing and returned to play their own instrument. As the drawing grew into a marvellous and comical creature, so the sound of the instruments grew in a shared regular rhythm. The results were artistically and musically amazing!

Recording sounds

Recording Wellie Wednesday sounds was introduced once the group had gelled. This was a cooperative group activity as it needed everyone to be completely quiet so that only the sounds being recorded could be heard, for example, the crackling fire, sausages sizzling, boots splashing in puddles and twigs being snapped. By recording the sounds with the group, it helped to trigger memories of their experiences and enabled them to reflect more vividly. After their sessions had finished, each child received a CD of the recorded sounds. This could be used as a soothing transitional object to facilitate calm moments.

Stretching lycra

Lycra was used in a similar way to using a parachute to develop cooperative circle games. Everyone held on to the edge of one large sheet of stretchy lycra material and games were played, sometimes including balls or toys bouncing in the middle. All worked together to achieve a common goal, for example, using the lycra to make big movements or small movements, violent waves or little ripples accompanied by a song. These activities required cooperation, holding still, quiet anticipation, being able to wait as the suspense built and they learnt to change between exuberant excitement and quiet calm.

Smile games

Find the smile: a smiley keyring was threaded onto a circle of thick string; the children kept the keyring hidden inside their hands as they passed it around the circle of string. One person, who stood in the middle watching, had to guess where the smile had ended up. In order to help guess, the person who held the keyring smiled, whilst everyone else tried to keep a straight face. This encouraged children to look and notice the expression of others.

Share a smile: children smiled at each other and their smile passed around the circle. For some children (see Chapter 4), smiling did not seem to come naturally, preferring to avoid eye contact; this was a good opportunity to practise within the group and recognise that smiles generate positive responses from others. One child returned the following week expressing surprise that his self-initiated smile at a teacher in the corridor had resulted in the teacher smiling back at him.

Learning to take turns

At each session there were times when children had to wait for a turn. This included taking turns to speak, to use equipment or to contribute to a game or an activity. Children were taught to be patient and to do 'good waiting' for their turn. Sometimes there were intentionally a limited number of resources available in order to create situations where sharing and taking turns were necessary, for example, a box with a limited number of bats and balls, one teaspoon to share between four for the 'cress egghead' activity. Children were encouraged to problem-solve and plan how to make it fair, for example, taking it in turns and watching each other.

Percussion instruments

The woodland creature activity previously described presented children with positive ways of taking turns. They enjoyed the fact that they could choose whose turn would be next. They noticed that everyone eventually got a turn and no-one was left out, because at the end everyone was playing their chosen instrument, showing that they had all contributed to the drawing of the creature.

Conversations through the use of percussion instruments allowed children to take turns in taking the lead. Working in pairs, adult with child, one partner initiated a rhythm and the other replied, taking turns. For one child, giving up the lead in other situations was hard, but during this game with percussion instruments he easily gave up the lead and followed someone else's rhythm pattern. He suddenly realised that without using words they were taking turns being the leader and the follower.

Lining up

Some children had repeatedly demonstrated a need to be at the front of a line of children when they were in school. Not being first had triggered anger or refusal. This was discussed in terms of taking turns to be at the front; games were introduced to practise being in various positions in a line: at the front, middle and back. Starting in a line, the children were shown that if the line joined up they could make new shapes, for example, circle or square. The circle could then separate in different places to make new lines, for example, parallel lines, lines facing in different directions, shorter lines, and as result, new 'leaders' would automatically emerge. This game allowed them to change positions and still feel OK, wherever they were, realising that it was fair.

Encouraging cooperation and empathy

For some children, working together cooperatively can be a challenge, particularly if they have a competitive spirit. One particular child arrived at the first Wellie Wednesday session with a strong need to win; to be first and quicker than everyone else (see Chapter 13). Through the activities, he was encouraged, along with the rest of the group, to cooperate, to cheer others on to do their best and to celebrate the achievements of others. As mentioned before, when two children both had the same idea, or both had the right answer to a question, they were encouraged to celebrate with thumbs up and say 'Great minds think alike' rather than 'he stole my idea' or 'I thought of that first'.

In order to cooperate, children need to have a degree of empathy, they need to be able to tune into others and understand how they are feeling. Gradually, with practice, they can develop the language of empathy and express their understanding of, and concerns for, others. Throughout the sessions they were encouraged to be kind to each other and to work together to keep everyone safe.

Children cooperating through play

Through play in the early years, children gradually progress from independent play, to playing side by side with others, then gradually to playing with others and cooperating. For children involved in the project it was important to progress through these stages, gradually encouraging them to share, take turns and collaborate. As the weeks progressed, relationships were built and children began to interact positively with each other.

They were increasingly given more opportunities for free play that involved sharing and taking turns with equipment, taking responsibility for themselves and for what was fair. They began to recognise that cooperative play and activities with others could contribute to their own enjoyment. One child was delighted when others joined in with the plan he initiated of making a pile of leaves and taking turns to jump in it.

Children cooperating together, sharing the load

During the project, children experienced having a common goal, achieving in collaboration with others. Through a range of planned activities children began to realise that there were some things they could not achieve alone but could accomplish in collaboration with others. Children were given the opportunity to pull a heavy cart full of wood for the fire, and together they steered around obstacles and over bumpy ground. They took turns to be at the front and the back, using the language of negotiation, compromise and camaraderie.

Parents, carers and children working together in pairs

Children were given many opportunities to work with their own parent or carer, and sometimes also with another adult:

- Making 'egg heads': parents and carers were given stick-on eyes and pens to create faces on eggshells, which were then stuffed with cotton wool. The children placed cress seeds on top of the cotton wool to grow for the hair. Then they took turns to carefully carry water to the seeds with a teaspoon. By providing only one spoon they needed to watch each other, working together with care and concentration and enjoying the efforts of others.
- Pitching tents: at some sessions each pair pitched their own tents, which required cooperation and communication to agree on their strategies.
- Sand trays: children and adults took turns to make sand tray patterns or pictures in individual plastic trays, watching each other with attention and without interrupting concentration.
- Obstacle course: during one activity, adults wore a blindfold and children were asked to guide their partner around an obstacle course, holding their hands and speaking instructions. This introduced the opportunity to talk about trust.
- Woodland palettes: working together they made 'woodland palettes', collecting things from the ground and making patterns of colours on a piece of card shaped like a painting palette. Strips of double-sided tape had been stuck to the palette so that they could peel the backing off and attach their leaves and other treasures from the wood.
- Woodland faces: at the final sessions in a cleared area of ground in the woods, each pair created a woodland face. They collected twigs, leaves, stones, feathers, acorns and other things found on the ground and used these to create their face. When they had finished the group walked around together to admire and applaud each face to celebrate their success. The faces were left as a gift to the countryside.

Adults working together

Parents and carers often worked together assisting the cook in food preparation, talking with each other whilst preparing vegetables or chopping fruit. They worked as a group on a wide range of other activities as well, proudly showing the children their achievements at the end:

- Kite making using canes and plastic bin bags.
- Making a hanging mobile with pieces of wood, which required sanding, decorating, drilling and threading with string. They were very proud of their combined effort. Afterwards, they helped the children to make another mobile.
- Shelter building: a group of the adults were set the challenge to build a waterproof shelter in the woods with tarpaulin and ropes. When they had finished, they made a trail of twig arrows for the children to follow in order to find their shelter. Once found, the adults got into the shelter and the children and team members tested the shelter with buckets of water to see whether it was waterproof!

Whole group cooperation

At every session there were a range of activities shared by the whole group, which required cooperation and positive interaction from everyone. Whole group times around the fire and circle activities on the field required listening with attention and respecting each others' turn to speak. Mealtimes involved a cooperative effort with everyone helping to serve, clear away or wash and dry up. Compliments regularly focused upon and celebrated cooperation within the whole group and recognised each others' successes particularly when overcoming difficulties. Cooperation and empathy were underpinning foundations of the Wellie Wednesday project.

Developing self-worth

The main aim of the Wellie Wednesday project was to involve children, and their parents or carers in a carefully planned experience, which would change their thinking and help them to move forward. For many, the first thing that needed to change was their self-confidence. Various activities were designed, aiming to encourage them to see themselves as members of the group who were able to make a positive and valued contribution. Some children needed to find ways of expressing themselves clearly in order to feel understood and have their views valued; significant factors in building a positive sense of self. They were encouraged to extend single word answers by the team using full sentences. Gradually, the children's vocabulary was extended along with their thinking and the use of more complex sentences.

Compliments

At every session there was a compliments time, when all members of the group were complimented on something specific that they had done that day. The note-taker wrote compliments throughout the day, with suggestions from all the team; gradually, group members joined in with additional compliments for each other. The compliments were read out at final circle time, then typed up on small strips of paper, laminated and given to each member of the group the next week, to take home and keep. Parents and carers talked about putting these in a prominent place, for example, on the fridge, as a reminder of 'good news'. Children talked about complimenting their parents, carers and friends during the weeks between sessions and they had noticed a positive effect. Adults, by feeling the effect of receiving compliments, began to notice and comment on their children's small but positive actions. For some, being complimented proved to be an unfamiliar and positive emotional experience, for example, 'Thank you, you were a good volunteer for washing and drying up after breakfast', 'We liked the way you gave good encouragement to Evie when she was eating her lunch with a wobbly tooth', 'We noticed that you were good at taking turns'.

Specific praise

Specific praise was very closely linked to compliments but was more ongoing and focused on the children. The team paid attention to very small things that showed children were making thoughtful choices and praised them specifically: 'Your hands are being so careful with that little snail', rather than just saying 'Well done', or focusing on another child who was not being careful. Praise was used to reinforce the beliefs and let children know that positive actions, however small, received attention and recognition, whilst negative actions were often not commented on. It was important to provide a trickle of positive comments throughout the day, within hearing of the group, so that a positive atmosphere was created where everyone realised it is often the small things that count.

Using a mirror

A mirror was placed in the base of a gold box and the lid placed on top. The box was passed around the circle and the group were told: 'Look inside and see something very special, but don't tell anyone else what you see.' As they lifted the lid and looked inside, they saw their own reflection. It made them smile and they managed to not tell anyone else what was inside! For some children, this was a significant moment and they referred to it later on. When the children's memory books were assembled, a plastic mirror was stuck on one of the pages with a poem alongside. 'The person I'd most like to be, is someone by the name of ME.'

Recognising feelings of pride

'Princess Proud' was one of the Hope Family of tortoises who was introduced to encourage the group to think about their successes and achievements and feel proud of themselves. Often, there is a tendency to be self-critical, so this was about celebrating one's own successes and self-complimenting. The comment 'I expect you must have felt very proud' encouraged children to be able to say 'I felt proud!' when they were successful on subsequent occasions. Adults were also encouraged to celebrate their achievements, both during the sessions and at home. It was as important for the adults as it was for the children to have the experience of receiving compliments so that they could start to recognise their own success. This raised their own self-esteem and helped them to realise the importance of complimenting their children on what they were getting right, however small.

Becoming independent and taking responsibility

Some children found it hard to perform tasks independently of their parent or carer, relying on them for support (see Chapter 14). These children were quick to give up and ask for help rather than persist through difficulty and had learnt to expect that help would quickly be offered. If help is always on hand children can begin to feel helpless and when an adult is not there for support can become tearful, angry or frustrated.

Percy Persevere, Try and Yet

'Percy Persevere' was a member of the Hope Family of tortoises. He encouraged children to persist and continue to work independently when tasks felt hard. 'Try' and 'Yet' were other tortoises who encouraged children to keep trying in order to achieve. The phrases that went with them were 'Try my best and not give up' and 'I can't do it yet, if I try, soon I will be able to say I can'. Examples of activities where children learnt to persist included balance activities on logs and tree climbing. They were given instruction on how to keep themselves safe, but were encouraged to manage it themselves with an adult nearby. Other activities included making Viking braiding (using a hexagon of card and lengths of wool to make a braid), drawing activities and making a percussion instrument using cardboard tubes and boxes. They were given encouragement and explicit instruction or suggestions but encouraged to keep going independently, rather than having someone do the task for them. The week after Percy Persevere was introduced, Yan said: 'I'm not never going to give up on anything!'

Adults and children working together

Working on a task with other children's parents or carers helped children to take on more responsibility as they were removed from the usual situation, where they knew what to expect. The adults enjoyed working with each other's children and showed empathy, patience and understanding to the needs of the child they partnered.

Taking responsibility at mealtimes

At breakfast time, children were encouraged to help themselves to cereal and pour their own milk from a small jug making this easy to manage successfully. They were taught how to safely chop fruit, put it on a shared plate and pass it round to others. The cook and other adult helpers supported them to make their own beef burgers. They took responsibility for filling their adult's pancakes, checking first what they would like, then selecting the correct fillings and serving them. Children also took on responsibility for washing and drying up dishes when time allowed. Using plastic water carriers, pairs of children were shown how to collect cold water from the tap and carry it safely between them.

Tent time

Children were given a time after lunch to be alone in their tents, initially only for about ten minutes. They were given a range of calming activities, which they could enjoy independently. It was recognised as a quiet resting time to be alone and to allow their adults to have a quiet cup of tea and chat with other adults. For some adults this was a new experience as at home they had felt continually in demand, unable to have five minutes to themselves.

The children were given the responsibility for unloading their bag, arranging their tent, and at the end of the day packing all their belongings back into their bag. As they learnt to settle in to tent time independently they also became better at making use of free play times. These changed from being potentially argumentative times to opportunities for increased cooperation and the sharing of ideas.

Learning to manage feelings and behaviour

Comfortable and uncomfortable feelings*

(*based on Greenberg and Kusche 1995)

Some children experience their feelings as something not only beyond their control but often beyond that of the adults around them. They are then left with additional feelings of shame or fear that nothing can be done to change how they react. At Wellie Wednesday, by clarifying the nature and relationship of feelings, behaviour and thoughts, the group found there are better ways to express uncomfortable feelings. It was explained that:

- Feelings are signals the body gives us about how we are on the inside.
- Feelings come, we do not have control over the feelings that arrive.
- We can accept all feelings.
- Behaviour arises out of the feelings.
- Behaviour can be in our control.
- Some behaviour is OK and some behaviour is Not OK.
- Finding appropriate ways to respond to feelings is an important part of gaining self-control.
- Thoughts can influence feelings and behaviour.
- We can have helpful and unhelpful thoughts.
- The choice of which thoughts to dwell on are within our control.

An awareness that feelings come in different intensities can help to contain them before they escalate. A person who is frequently angry may never have considered the emotional build-up that can happen, for example, from mild irritation, annoyance, feeling cross to becoming angry. For some this will even result in out-of-control rage. These stages were made visual as stages on an old fashioned thermometer (one needs to be shown to children who live in the digital age!) and the mercury line was coloured by each individual child from pale to bright red. Younger children used pale blue turning to red. Clothes pegs could be used to clip onto the side at the appropriate place (see Chapter 11). The colouring in activity allowed time for reflection on each level and how it represented a feeling becoming more intense. Use of the word 'stronger' was avoided as it could be confused with physical strength, something many saw as a desirable quality. It was then possible to use the concept of 'staying out of the red'.

The intensity of feelings could be estimated on the scale so that children became aware of monitoring and thinking of ways to prevent their feelings taking over and resulting in unpleasant outcomes for themselves and others. Brainstorming 'helpful thinking' allowed children to invent their own solutions and develop self-calming strategies.

Gary, who struggled with outbursts of anger, said: 'Sometimes my strong feelings make other people feel sad. In my heart sometimes I have 'don't want to' feelings, they make me feel angry.' Gary used his own sign, moving his hand over his heart and up to his head to remind him to move his strong feeling to his thinking brain. As he did so, his worried face changed to smiling.

Is it worth it?

This phrase was taught along with the physical action of a shoulder shrug to exhale pent-up breath and aid calming. Gradually, children became able to use their new knowledge to watch out for feelings that were going to cause them trouble. One child said he had felt like hitting another who was being very annoying but he thought 'Is it worth it?' and decided 'No'. Another said she was feeling that her friend was being unfair about sharing, then she thought 'Is it worth it?' and decided she did not want to get cross, as this would have stopped her playing with her friend.

When a feeling had been contained by an 'OK' behaviour or a helpful thought it was important to reinforce the feeling of pride. In addition, children were encouraged to use the silent clap (finger and thumb together, under the desk) when they knew they were keeping their behaviour OK, even if they experienced feeling an uncomfortable feeling.

ELISE SAID: I've turned my uncomfortable feeling into a comfortable one.

Helpful or unhelpful thinking?

The idea of 'helpful or unhelpful thinking' was introduced to start thinking about discontent, complaining and the inability to enjoy the pleasures of the present moment. The idea of whether a glass is half full or half empty was discussed using two glasses with carefully measured identical amounts of liquid. Role play was used to either be looking forward to drinking more, for example, 'Mmm, this drink is so delicious I am glad I have not finished it yet', or regretting that soon it would be finished: 'I haven't got much left, this drink is too little, it doesn't last long.' Then naming the pleasurable experiences of enjoyment and anticipation, compared with the uncomfortable ones of regret and annoyance, enabled a further discussion of how the way an event is viewed can lead to comfortable feelings or to uncomfortable feelings. Exploring the link between thoughts and feelings started with remembering that feelings arise, we do not necessarily choose them, but what we do with the feelings can lead to OK or Not OK behaviour. However, it is possible to make a decision about the ensuing behaviour.

Sometimes our thoughts can help us deal with uncomfortable feelings (we call this helpful thinking). At other times our thoughts can increase uncomfortable feelings or lead to Not OK behaviour (we call this unhelpful thinking). 'Is that helpful or unhelpful thinking?' became a question that the children were encouraged to use when getting into a negative state of mind. A team member would ask this question when a choice was being made based on unhelpful thinking.

Some children were quick to offload blame onto others, especially their parent or carer, for example, for what has been forgotten in their school bag rather than accepting responsibility themselves. By linking thoughts, feelings and behaviour the children started to realise that it is not necessarily others who cause uncomfortable feelings to arise but rather what choice is made when an unfavourable situation arises. Liam was overheard saying to himself:

> I don't want to do this but I'll do it anyway.

Some traditional tales were useful in reinforcing and exploring issues around feelings, thoughts and behaviour. The story of the Old Woman in the Vinegar Bottle is a good example (Fisher 1996). Every time the old woman is granted a wish to live somewhere better she soon bemoans the fact that her new home is not even bigger and better. The story makes clear that in some cases the option to enjoy the moment may lead to better feelings and experiences than complaining about what has happened or what cannot be attained. This idea was helpful when encouraging children to attempt a challenging task. Whenever the response from a child was 'I can't' they were reminded that 'can't' was unhelpful thinking, it stopped their brain getting ready to have a go. It can be unhelpful to say 'I can't' as this engenders feelings of defeat and no hope, therefore, the effort does not seem worthwhile. It is more helpful and motivating to say 'I can't do it YET', which sends a message of expectation that 'soon I will be able to say I can'.

One teacher extended this idea, responding to any further negativity by suggesting: 'Well you could pretend that you can, and have a go.'

> I can't do it YET
> But if I TRY MY BEST
> And PRACTISE
> Soon I will be able to say
> I CAN.

Not my favourite thing

When children were reluctant to eat and prone to saying 'I don't like it', whether they had tried it or not, they were encouraged to use helpful thinking in the form of 'Its not my favourite thing but I'll try it' (our thanks to volunteer Pippa Sayers). This phrase helped to defuse potentially stressful mealtimes, which some families had been experiencing. Emma's mother told us that when Emma saw it was lasagne she started to complain, then she remembered and said, 'It's not my favourite thing' and proceeded to eat two helpings! (see Chapter 15).

Silent speech bubble

For some children the urge to talk incessantly or to call out, interrupt or want to answer all questions was a frustrating difficulty in school (see Chapter 7). Children needed help to understand that feeling they want to speak is OK but only at an appropriate time. A visual aid was used to develop the concept of keeping the words inside your head. An empty speech bubble represented no words being said aloud. Through the use of the 'Voices' song, children were encouraged to think words but keep them in their head. This song uses different voices and ends with a thinking voice where the children have to think the final verse but not sing the words aloud (see Chapter 8).

When you ... I feel ... because ...

When situations arose where one person caused another to feel an emotion, they were encouraged to use 'I feel ...' language. Modelling this with comfortable feelings helped to familiarise children with the idea that words and actions impact on the feelings of others. 'When you helped me put the chairs out I felt pleased because it made the job easier with two of us.' 'When you arrived with big smiles I felt excited because I knew you were happy to be here.' 'When you moved up to make room for everyone to fit onto the bench I felt proud of you because you were being kind and thoughtful to others.' Using 'I feel ...' language when the feelings were uncomfortable allowed children to express how they felt rather than make accusations. Accusations are likely to exacerbate confrontational behaviour, whereas hearing how someone is being made to feel is more likely to lead to an apology or a change in the behaviour.

It is not apparent to young children that others may feel differently to them. Learning that another person may be upset by something they have no concern over, and hearing how others feel, improves their understanding and leads to the development of empathy. 'I felt upset when you pushed me because it hurt.' 'I felt annoyed when you took the ball I was playing with because you didn't ask if you could play with me.' 'I feel fed up when you always want to use the mouse and I just have to watch because it's not fair.'

Triggers

Feelings are triggered by many situations and experiences, for example, transition between activities, close proximity of others, fear of the unknown. There may be physical triggers, as identified in Maslow's hierarchy of needs, such as hunger, thirst, being too hot or cold. Helping children to identify what triggers uncomfortable feelings can give them insight and may allow them to avert behaviour that is unacceptable to others. Ned told us that when his younger brother was being annoying he used to hit him but now he was able to move away. He described it as having a firework inside him but instead of exploding he stopped it from igniting by moving away. He said he now told his big sister: 'I am feeling annoyed so keep away from me.'

Many children experienced frightening times of out-of-control anger. They needed to understand that anger can be triggered by many different feelings. By asking themselves 'What am I really feeling?' (for example, worry, fear, sadness, upsetting thoughts, frustration, annoyance), it is possible to reduce their anxieties around feeling angry. It was explained that anger is a justifiable feeling and it is recognised that containing it can be difficult. However, it is like any other feeling in that acting in anger can lead to OK or Not OK behaviour. Children were encouraged to think about what behaviour would be acceptable if they felt angry. They suggested moving away, calming breathing, cuddling their special toy or going to their safe place.

It was also kept in mind that there are a range of deep-seated causes which can result in challenging or unacceptable behaviour. The aim was to try to identify and address the source of the emotional response rather than focusing on managing the anger. Children can be supported by:

- Teaching calming strategies for anxiety driven anger.
- Using relevant stories to address the impact of bereavement and loss.
- Using narrative conversations to externalise a problem.
- Experiencing a culture of kindness to replace aggressive attitudes.
- Naming feelings, e.g., jealousy, loneliness, worry.
- Creating reassuring routines and responses for fear-driven anger.
- Following safeguarding guidelines in cases where the identified cause is abuse.

Accepting mistake making

Fear of making mistakes can cause some children to opt out, refuse to start work, destroy work or distract from the task with disruptive behaviour. For some, punishment for getting things wrong has shaped their fear of attempting new things. For others, a perfectionist attitude causes them to feel mistakes are unacceptable. Successful thinking and learning requires formulating ideas, testing, then adapting them to accommodate new information. Adults modelling problem-solving by thinking aloud helped to demonstrate that when something goes wrong a new solution can usually be found:

> We have walked down the field and I said that we would climb the stile but the cows have made it so muddy and slippery I think I will change the plan and we will walk through the wood to the gate and get to the stream across the other field.

> Because the bus got held up we are later than usual so won't have time for everything we planned. To catch up today we will leave the breakfast washing up to do later with the lunch things.

Check and change*

(*This phrase name is taken from Lake, M., and Needham, M., (1995). Imaginative minds)
'Check' and 'Change' were the names of two of the Hope Family characters. They were used to overcome defeatism by encouraging the idea that if something is not working then changing to a different way of doing it may be a good solution. Praise was given when a child was seen to change how they were doing something. 'Well done I saw you "check and change" when you tried to squeeze through the gap and couldn't fit so you went another way.' 'Good thinking, I noticed you used "check and change" when you were counting the cups and got in a muddle and started again.'

Having experienced praise for self-correcting, children responded to a quick reminder to 'check and change' when mistakes were made, for example, pushing into the middle of the dinner queue: 'Uh oh, I think you need to "check and change", you should be at the back.' Hearing others congratulated, even though they had made a mistake, was a new experience and, for the timid, it encouraged them to have a go. For the perfectionists, 'check and change' enabled them to make mistakes without losing face.

Secondary behaviour

Sometimes, when given an instruction, a child may attempt to create a diversion by making excuses or grumbling. This is called secondary behaviours, the primary behaviour being to follow the instruction.

As challenging behaviour escalates it is easy for staff to become engaged in inadvertently fuelling the secondary behaviour. When an unacceptable behaviour has occurred it is best to focus upon the required primary behaviour. A calm straightforward instruction needs to be given: 'Matt, you need to come back to your seat and get on with your work.' If, as he returns to his work he swears, complains about being picked on and thumps the table, this is not the moment to comment because he is following the instruction to return. As soon as possible praise should be given, for example, 'Well done for getting started Matt.' If attention had been given to his secondary behaviour, it is very likely to increase the undesirable behaviour because the signal has been sent that it has gained attention. Conversely, by praising a positive behaviour it is more likely to be repeated.

Building trust to support change and transition

Some children experience severe anxiety when they are unsure of what will happen next. They ask for details of what will happen and when, for example, 'When will we eat?' They are unable to bear the unknown and will ask continually about the next activity. Some demonstrate anxiety at change over times, moving from one activity to another; endings also trigger anxiety for fear of what will happen next. This can be communicated through the children's behaviour; they may not be aware of what is causing the anxiety and may not be able to verbalise their feelings. Their behaviour may become antisocial, aggressive or tearful; they may refuse to respond to requests or run to what they consider to be a safe place, for example, under a table.

Five minute warnings

It helps children to know that the end of an activity is approaching: 'In five minutes we are going to do this', 'You need to be finishing off now ready to stop in three minutes' (sand timers can provide a further visual warning). At Wellie Wednesday these warnings were given when activities were about to end and a change was going to happen. A routine was established for the end of the day so that children knew the day was drawing to a close: final circle, compliments, sharing beautiful thoughts around a candle and farewell. A butterfly chart was introduced to visually show the children how many sessions were left before the end of their turn at Wellie Wednesday.

This was extended for one child in school to help her understand how long the holiday would be before she returned to school.

Reassurance through structure

A visual timetable was used on a laminated sheet to show children and adults that there was a consistent routine to the day each week at Wellie Wednesday. Other activities were introduced by attaching extra unlabelled pictures to the chart. The children were encouraged to wait and see and to trust the adults that all would be well, they would find out later what the activities would be.

Expectations were made clear: children were expected to follow instructions, trusting the adults to keep them safe, for example, a clear explanation of rules for walking in the woods was given before entering the woods. Expectations were consistent and were repeated, often using the beliefs chart as calm reminders, so a raised voice was not needed.

Two good choices

Offering the children two good choices provides a secure structure, which allows them to make a choice within the expectations. 'Would you like to sit on the bench or on the chair?' is more effective than 'Sit down' or 'Where would you like to sit?' when a child is having difficulty settling. Other examples are: 'Can you do it alone or would you like me to help you?', 'Are you going to finish your work now or when the others go to lunch?'

Being held in mind, not being forgotten

For some children, physical closeness to a significant adult provides their security and reassurance. Because this is not always possible, it is important for these children to understand that they are kept in mind and not forgotten. They will feel reassured by an adult saying, 'I haven't forgotten you, I will come back to you later.' An object belonging to an adult can help to ease the separation, such as holding their teacher's pen or, keeping a parent's key fob in their school bag or pocket. When walking in the woods there were some children who thrived on being trusted to take care of something belonging to the adult; the notion of trust was discussed and one child said, 'You trusted me didn't you?'

A regular task for which a child is responsible helps them to feel remembered, such as 'Billie will chop up the fruit next Wednesday', being careful to remember to always follow this through.

Soothing, calming and reassuring

Many of the children referred from school for this project were impulsive in their thinking and behaviour. In school, difficulties often arose because of their reactive responses to many situations. It was our belief that challenging and aggressive behaviour was often driven by high anxiety, a state that diminishes the ability to think rationally. For some children, it seemed that chronic anxiety and hyper-alert reactions were their predominant state of being. Parents and carers too were often highly stressed so for the whole group it was important to build times into the day for practising calming activities. At the start of a calming time it was important to bring the body under control so that quiet sitting could be achieved. Stillness requires more muscular control than movement, developmentally coming later than control of gross motor movements. A few coordination exercises were used to gain attention and focus.

Coordination exercise: crossovers

Standing with feet slightly apart use the right hand to touch the left ear, put right hand down. Use the left hand to touch the right ear, put the left hand down, continue down the body using each hand in turn to touch the *opposite* side of the body naming the parts:

> Shoulder shoulder
> Waist waist
> Knee knee
> Toe toe
> Heel heel (bending the leg behind the standing leg to enable this and to require balance)

Then repeat reversing the order. It is important to explain that this needs to be done slowly and carefully in order to maintain balance and precision. Rushing through does not serve to calm but is easier than concentrating on each movement. Think of how riding a bicycle as slowly as possible is harder than going faster. This seemingly simple exercise is very exacting for many children as it requires concentration, balance, crossing over the mid-line and memorising a sequence. However, it always seems to spark a desire for mastery, so is a very good starting point for explaining how satisfaction is felt when something that was difficult at first can, with practice, become easy. This then allows a golden opportunity for bridging (see Chapter 18), discussing where else could knowing about mastery of challenge be useful? Increasing the difficulty of the challenge can be achieved once mastered, by:

- Naming of the body part being touched can be replaced with counting to add a further challenge.
- Counting backwards whilst reversing the actions to get back to one as the left ear is touched.
- Completing the whole sequence with eyes shut.
- Reciting a rhyme or poem whilst completing the actions.
- Using a foreign language to count and name the body parts.

Calming techniques: Balancing rainbows

A second exercise was used to encourage deep breaths, which in themselves have a calming effect. Deep breathing activates the parasympathetic nervous system by moving out of the threat/drive sympathetic system. Standing with feet slightly apart for good balance, move the palms of the hands together in front of the body then slowly upwards breathing in until they are together above the head. Exhaling slowly, move the arms outwards to the sides making a rainbow shape above the head. Repeat three times. This is a quietening set of movements in preparation for dropping the arms to the side and concentrating on the breathing only.

Calming techniques: 7/11 breathing

Breathe in through the nose to the count of seven, hold for one. Breathe out through the mouth to the count of eleven. This requires controlled exhaling to make the breath last for the full count. Initially, lower counts need to be used to develop the technique. This exercise ensures emptying of the lungs so countering the shallow breathing that is often prevalent when people feel anxious. It is also beneficial in that it lowers, and therefore relaxes, the shoulders, which then releases tension in the neck.

Calming techniques: guided visualisation

The Rainbow Garden (a guided visualisation) was used to aid developing soothing feelings, which the children could then access at other times; many told us of using it to help them get to sleep at night. Children were taught that they have a part of the mind that is called the imagination. It allows us to think about things that have not really happened, things that are not real and to explore new ideas and rehearse how things might be. For some troubled children, entering the realm of the imagination does not feel safe and can release frightening and disturbing thoughts. For this reason they are afraid of silence and being alone with their thoughts. A carefully guided visualisation was used to ensure that only good safe and calming experiences were imagined.

> A Beautiful Garden: A Special Place
> Adapted from ideas by J. Day (1994)
>
> In your head start to use your imagination to find a path … walk along it and as you do notice what it is like. Maybe it is grassy or stony, winding or straight … there could be fields or woods on each side of your path. Then as you look ahead you see that there are some Rainbow Tortoise Twins waiting either side of a gate … there is a rainbow above the gate for you to walk under.
>
> Take a minute to look at the gate. What is it like? Is it wooden or metal? What colour is it? Maybe it is old and rickety or perhaps new and shiny. Is it a special shape? Look carefully as you walk up to it.
>
> The gate is not quite shut and the Rainbow Twins invite you to go through. Inside you find yourself in a beautiful garden. What do you see and hear? Maybe you can smell beautiful flowers? Perhaps there are birds singing. You might see colourful butterflies.
>
> As you look about you hear the sound of running water. Look around to see where the sound is coming from. Is it a stream, a waterfall, a fountain, a pond or a lake? When you have found it, take time to just enjoy watching it.
>
> As you look around you see a special place to sit where you can look out on the whole garden. What sort of place have you found? Maybe a hidden den or a tree house, perhaps it is under a tree in the shade. Sit comfortably in your own special place.

As you sit there you will notice something else, something especially for you. It might be something you see, a lovely sound that you listen to, or the smell of the flowers. Maybe it is some juicy fruit growing for you to pick. Whatever it is that makes you feel so special to be in this beautiful place, feel calm and peaceful as you enjoy it.

Now it is time for you to return to the gate so get up from your special sitting place and walk back across the garden, taking a good look as you go. When you reach the gate, go through, close it behind you and say thank you to the Rainbow Twins.

Look back knowing you can come again to the beautiful garden whenever you like. It is always peaceful and always safe.

Walk back along the path and feel glad that you have a special place for beautiful thoughts.

The visualisation was used for some children in one-to-one follow-up sessions in school. For use with other children, the type of creature used can be changed, for example, butterflies. If children included threatening images, e.g. monsters or guns, they would be told this is not the special place that is the Rainbow Garden and be encouraged to try again. Some children liked to talk about what they had seen during the visualisation, some liked to dictate their thoughts then keep a copy. One child, who despite going through very difficult times, dictated this (and gave permission to share it):

My Beautiful Garden is very precious, the gate is made in the shape of a butterfly. The Rainbow Twins were painting it lots of different colours. Inside it was very short grass and not many flowers yet. The water in it was a pretty waterfall with butterflies flying around. I sat on a butterfly-shaped bench just for one person to sit on. One day it will be painted just for me. My special treat was a butterfly that looked like a bird. It landed on my arm. Before I saw it I thought there is nothing here for me. Then I heard Percy Persevere, he said 'Don't worry there's obviously something here for you. The Rainbow Twins wouldn't bring you here for no reason.' Then there it appeared.

Calming techniques: beautiful thoughts time

As mentioned previously it was important to end every Wellie Wednesday day calmly, and with an opportunity to be reflective. At the final circle and compliments time a bag was passed round. In it was a small item of interest or an object related to the day's activities or sometimes something for each group member to take home, for example, a tiny tortoise (after introducing Wise and Little Turtle), a polished stone (after using the sand trays), a laminated smile picture (after learning the smile games). This was done in silence and each person kept the surprise hidden from others to build up the feelings of anticipation and cooperation.

The lighting of the candle in the Circle of Friends candle holder followed this and in a minute of silence everyone was invited to listen to the surrounding sounds of nature and think a beautiful thought. The team shared their thoughts and others gradually felt comfortable to join in. Contributing their ideas to the group at the end of the minute was optional.

Calming techniques: tent time

Some told us that their children were reluctant to be on their own and found it difficult to occupy themselves. They were also often difficult to settle at night. In order to foster a positive attitude to time spent alone, 'tent time' was a routine part of the day. After lunch, the children went to their own tent and were expected to stay in it until the next group activity. They were able to snuggle down and rest as they had fleecy blankets and a special cushion each. At the start of the project they were also given a 'tent friend', usually a soft toy puppy. They named it and knew it would be waiting for them each week. Tent activities were also provided: books, puzzles, paper and pencil if they wanted to use them.

Despite the excitement of having a tent of their own, staying in it for ten minutes was at first very difficult. In some cases, a staff member initially needed to sit nearby without engaging in conversation but to be a reassuring presence, encouraging the children to stay in their tent. They were told that their tent time was a time to experience privacy (see Chapter 18). It explaining that it was also the grown-ups' time. It was made clear that they did not have to sleep or shut the tent door but they did have to remain quiet and enjoy time to themselves.

Calming techniques: transitional objects

Facts about the necessity of sleep for healthy body and brain development were explained. Children learnt about nocturnal animals needing to be awake at night. They drew pictures of them on pillow cases to remind them that night time was sleep time for children.

Once soothing routines, calming exercises and experiences of the associated comfortable feelings had become established, it was important to ensure that memories of these transferred from the outdoor day to home and school. The laminated compliments slips given out each week, the small objects referred to earlier, and a goodbye card reminding them that we looked forward to seeing them again next week, were all designed to keep them engaged with what they had learnt and the associated comfortable feelings.

At the end of each group's six weeks they took home their special tent time friend and a carefully compiled memories book containing reminders of all the activities, stories, strategies they had encountered, as well as plenty of photographs and copies of all their compliments. On the last week they decorated a handkerchief, which was then hung over the fire. When presented to them at the final circle in a sealed polythene bag they were amazed to open it and smell Wellie Wednesday! One child took this to school in his bag and said he went to sniff it sometimes when he felt worried. Another child took her puppy-shaped bag to school and was allowed to fetch it and hang it on the back of her chair when her uncomfortable feelings were escalating. The action of going to fetch it served as a distracting activity, removing her temporarily, resulting in her feelings becoming more manageable. She said: 'Puppy helped me, no hurting this week, my hands are kind hands now. The feelings have gone. I feel excited I am not hurting anymore. I love Puppy.' Through using the above strategies, children calmed and connected, parents and carers were able to relax and enjoy the company of others.

Adults were given laminated inspirational sayings, reminders of Wellie Wednesday sayings and memos of any parenting tips discussed. All group members received something to take home as a reminder of the day. This was another way to reinforce a sense of belonging that could act as a source of strength to tap back into during the week ahead.

The underpinning beliefs that were set out at the start of each group session became embedded in the minds of all who took part. The strategies described in this chapter helped to put these beliefs into practice:

> We are kind to each other.
> We follow instructions.
> We keep ourselves and each other safe.
> We look after the Wellie Wednesday environment.

Sammy, one year later, told a team member who was visiting him at his new school: 'I still say the beliefs but not the Wellie Wednesday environment now'. This thoughtful comment led to changing the wording to: 'We look after the environment', so that it was more transferable to school and home settings.

Reflection

How can simple guidelines be established to make explicit what is important in any chosen setting? Why does this make a difference?

References

Day, J. (1994). *Creative visualization for children: A practical guide*. Shaftesbury: Element Books.

Greenberg, M. and Kusche, C. (1995). *Promoting alternative thinking strategies (PATHS)*. South Deerfield: Channing Bete.

Lake, M., and Needham, M., (1995) *Imaginative Minds*. Birmingham, UK: Imaginative Minds.

Chapter 17

Supporting parents and carers

Don't walk behind me, I may not lead.
Don't walk in front of me, I may not follow.
Just walk beside me...

(Albert Camus)

It took an enormous amount of organisation, time and energy for parents and carers to be able to attend the sessions, juggling other children, jobs and their own anxieties about a day in the countryside with, initially at least, a group of strangers. To commit to doing this was an indication of the importance they attached to helping their child.

Initial interviews always made clear to them that their role in each session was one of encourager, enabler and companion in having fun and celebrating success. They were reassured that they were not expected to cope with any negative behaviour their child might display, so there would be no humiliating scenes of a parent or carer struggling with their child.

The team were experienced in engaging with challenging, disruptive and withdrawn children so it was agreed that they would always be on hand to guide and support the parents and carers and to step in if necessary. In this way, adults saw others modelling effective ways of working with non-compliance, disruption and children's disagreements.

The emphasis was on helping the adults to be encouraging, to praise and to compliment the children on all they were getting right. It was therefore important that any frustrations and anxieties about their child's experiences during the week were not expressed openly in front of the children. Group time was for hearing good news. A separate 20–30-minute time each week, away from the children, was devoted to discussion with parents and carers about their causes for concern. This required a carefully planned and mediated format to prevent the development of a spiralling catalogue of worse case scenarios.

A solution-focused approach was used, always bringing the discussion back to what had worked previously, whilst using the examples shared to introduce parenting skills strategies.

Parents and carers were also able to have further one-to-one conversations by phone if they needed extra support whilst putting into practice a new idea. Those who were unable to attend for family or health reasons were also phoned regularly to keep them updated of progress and to help them take on the successful strategies that their children were experiencing. Telephone contact was also used in exceptional cases of high need in order to prevent an imminent permanent exclusion or breakdown of an in-care placement. Support and catch up phone calls continued after the six-week attendance had been completed. Continuing contact was essential to support parents, carers and schools in maintaining success.

Topics covered during weekly discussions with the parents and carers fell into five areas.

Giving attention

Understanding that giving attention to a behaviour increases the likelihood of that behaviour being repeated. Attention is a survival need, babies who fail to get attention would die, so the brain is ever-alert to finding ways of receiving it.

It is up to the adults to shape the behaviour they want to see more of by attending to them with positive reactions. Likewise, they need to be able to ignore low-level negative behaviour in order to prevent them becoming a child's habitual mode of being noticed.

Thinking of behaviour as falling into three categories was encouraged:

1. Behaviour requiring **praise**: getting it right.

   By noticing and commenting in front of the child, for example, 'It was great that you did all that on your own', 'Well done for waiting quietly while I was on the phone', 'Thank you for hanging your coat up', the focus remained positive. Sometimes adults would feel that when children do the right thing it is to be expected and praise is therefore not necessary. Each week as adults and children alike were complimented, thanked and praised for their contributions they were able to experience first-hand how praise feels and how motivating it can be.

2. Behaviour to **ignore/distract**: low-level disruption, annoying behaviour designed to catch the eye, senseless comments.

   To get involved in trying to stop this behaviour is more likely to result in them escalating as the child has sensed they are gaining attention. Distraction often works well at these times, 'Oh look, I can see a … out of the window' or wondering aloud, 'I wonder whether … is on TV tonight?' or involving them in a new activity, 'I need some help to set the table now, what do we need to do first?'

3. Dangerous behaviour that needs to **stop**.

   There is a clear distinction between a behaviour that can cause an accident and one that is designed to provoke reaction. When STOP is required an adult must give a clear instruction as to what is required, then ensure it is followed. 'Stop! You need to put that down now, it could hurt someone, we need to keep everyone safe.'

Parents and carers were often surprised how effectively praise worked despite at first being accused of 'talking funny' by their children. They also found it useful to have become familiar with the 'Wise Turtle's target chart', which gave them ideas of small things to praise, for example, good sitting.

Giving instructions

The adults were helped to see that a clear instruction is easier for a child to follow than a negative comment made in response to a behaviour. Processing language is required; a child has to think what the words mean then reinterpret them to grasp what was meant. Say what you want, not what you don't want. It was pointed out to the adults that comments made sarcastically are too difficult for most young children to unravel. If they use sarcasm, this may result in their child misunderstanding and doing exactly what they did not want them to do. Children are likely to hear the words and act on them. 'Don't run' is likely to be interpreted as 'run', the last word heard. The adults liked the example of negative thinking used to demonstrate, 'Don't think about yellow … call out the name of the first fruit you think of.' It was inevitably bananas! Children were given precise directions. Instead of 'don't spill' and 'stop pushing', 'Tip the jug slowly and carefully to pour out the water' and 'Put your hands by your side and your feet flat on the ground while you line up.' 'Let's …' or 'Shall we …?' questions to preface what is being said should only be used when a genuine choice is on offer. It is no good asking a child if they want to do something if what is really meant is 'this needs to happen now', for example, 'It's time to get in the car now', rather than 'Shall we get in the car now?'

Feelings language

The naming of feelings was found to be helpful. Parents and carers were often surprised to find that if they acknowledged what their child had said by linking it to a feeling it was often enough to de-escalate a situation. 'I can see you are feeling annoyed but you still need to pick your coat up off the floor', 'I know you are feeling disappointed that we can't go to the park tonight.' They were also able to use this to good effect when their children were arguing with each other and wanted a parent or carer to take sides. 'I can see you are annoyed with each other but we need to talk about what we can do about it.'

Bedtime routines

A recurring concern was the difficulty experienced in getting their children to go to and stay in bed. Discussion of bedtime routines emphasised the importance of sleep. Giving parents and carers factual information encouraged them to explain to their children that brains and bodies need sleep in order to grow and function well. Often, bedtimes were seen as a power struggle. Giving a reason as to why sleep is necessary enabled the adults to ensure that their children got enough sleep. The knowledge of the science behind sleep enabled them to feel more confident when addressing their children. This, in turn, served to defuse the anger and distress previously involved at bedtimes.

As has been previously mentioned, 'Grown-up time' was a concept that the children were introduced to during sessions. This was a time when they were expected to go to their tents and quietly amuse themselves whilst the parents, carers and a team member met. Changing the language to change the behaviour was often successful and parents found that they were able to incorporate the same expectations and use of grown-up time at bedtimes. Having to go to sleep is impossible to enforce and can set up anxiety around not being able to get to sleep. It is easier for a child to learn to stay quietly resting. This is in itself a precursor to falling asleep. Parents and carers found that they could successfully use: 'You need to stay in bed and rest, it is grown-up time downstairs now.'

Some parents and carers observed that the later it gets, the more hyperactive their child becomes. Being over-tired requires increased motor movement and activity to maintain a wakeful state. Children who appear not to be tired are often over-tired but lacking in the ability to calm themselves in order to reach a sleepy state. Introducing calming routines was therefore an important change that the adults made. 'Winding down time' for half an hour before bed required reducing motor activity and the use of stimulating DVDs and computer games. Ideally, it would include looking at books, listening to stories, and having a drink of warm milk to ensure they were not going to sleep on an empty stomach. This routine gives a child some close enjoyable time with their parent or carer along with the soothing effect of a warm drink. It was sometimes necessary to point out that caffeinated sugary drinks act as stimulants and will making falling asleep more difficult. Caffeine found in tea, coffee, Coca-Cola and chocolate, acts as a block to adenosine, a neuro transmitter made in the brain. One of the functions of adenosine is to induce drowsiness in preparation for sleep. Studies show that caffeine breakdown in the body during the night is implicated in increasing the number of wakeful periods experienced. This is thought to be because it prevents entering the deeper stages of the sleep cycle.

A common practice seemed to be keeping a light on in the bedroom along with use of light emitting TV, computer and phone screens. The adults found it helpful to understand the effects of light on the quality of sleep achieved and the implications. With factual information backing them up, they were better able to set boundaries, rather than feeling weakened by their children's arguments. Apart from light making falling asleep at night more difficult, long-term studies indicate that without sufficient darkness the body's ability to manufacture the brain hormone melatonin is impaired. Melatonin is required to regulate body temperature, blood pressure and glucose levels.

Human givens approach

The human givens approach (Griffin and Tyrrell 2003) to meeting basic needs was derived from Maslow's hierarchy (Maslow 1954; see Chapter 18). Maslow believed that until the primary needs were met, the higher-level needs could not be accessed. Everyone has emotional needs, but also innate resources to help meet those needs. Exploration and identification of unfulfilled needs helped parents and carers to identify gaps for themselves as well as their children.

To make self-assessment easier, some key questions were used to initiate a discussion. The following areas of need were listed for consideration with linked statements for each parent or carer to consider and complete for their child:

- Safeness and security: I feel safe when …
- Attention: Someone who notices me is …
- Emotional connection: … is important in my life.
- Control/autonomy: I like being able to … by myself.
- Connection to wider community: One thing I can do to make my school a good place is …
- Achievement/competence: Something I am proud of is …
- Status/acceptance: … likes me because …
- Being valued: I feel special because …
- Privacy/time: I like spending time on my own doing …
- Space: A place I feel safe is …
- Meaning/challenge: Something I did that was difficult was …
- Responsibility: Something I can be trusted to do is …
- Purpose/belief system: One thing I believe is really important is … ; Something that would make the world a better place is …

The adults also soon began to relate the statements to themselves and clearly saw the areas of need within their own experience. This activity proved a constructive way for them to start making changes for their family's preferred future.

A chart of concentric circles divided into segments was devised. Each area of need was coded with a colour and the adults were asked to colour as much of each section of the circle as they felt was representative of how well each need was being met. The use of the chart and accompanying specific sentences created a focus and suggested ideas for discussion. These starting points offered a non-threatening structure, which encouraged a relaxed opportunity for talking. For example, one mother on looking at the chart, immediately exclaimed, 'I can't colour in anything for Privacy, I don't get any time to myself.' Another mother, when thinking about the autonomy section, recognised that she never expected her son to take any responsibility. She felt unable to let him have a go in case her own high standards were not achieved. Others commented that: 'It is quicker and easier to do it myself.' The chart was used as a tool in the family discussion with children about being aware of each other's needs and it generated change in their family life.

At all times the aim was to work alongside the parents and carers in a safe and supportive setting, offering them a range of strategies from which we hoped they would find ways to feel more secure in their parental roles.

> Behavior in the human being is sometimes a defense, a way of concealing motives and thoughts.
> The fact is that people are good. Give people affection and security and they will give affection and be secure in their feelings and their behavior.
>
> (Abraham Maslow)

Reflection

How can staff ensure that parents and carers feel sufficiently comfortable and welcome in school so that they can share positive attitudes about learning with their children.

Chapter 18

The theoretical background

Putting theory into practice

Everyone can learn, can change.

(Reuven Feuerstein)

It was important to be able to base our ways of working and the content we delivered on firm foundations. We needed to ensure that the Wellie Wednesday curriculum was securely based in well-founded and well-researched theory. This chapter aims to give an overview of the evidence-based theoretical background we found helpful when delivering a specialised curriculum to vulnerable children and their parents or carers.

Maslow's hierarchy of needs

Maslow's hierarchy of needs has already been mentioned in the introduction (see Figure 1.1), but further information is included here.

> Let people realise clearly that every time they threaten someone, humiliate or hurt unnecessarily, or dominate or reject another human being, they become forces for the creation of psychopathology even if these be small forces. Let them realise that every human being who is kind, hopeful, decent, psychologically warm is a psychotherapeutic force, even though a small one.
>
> (Maslow 1954)

Abraham Maslow (1908–1970) believed that humans naturally tend towards emotional growth and love, being motivated by having the following basic needs that must be satisfied:

- Physiological: hunger, thirst, physical comfort.
- Safety: security, out of danger, no need to be in a state of hyper vigilance 'on guard'.
- Belonging: love, acceptance, identification with others.
- Esteem: approval, recognition, competence, achievement.
- Self-actualisation: acceptance of self and others, respect.

Later, he further categorised two levels prior to self-actualisation:

- Cognitive: to know, understand and explore.
- Aesthetic: appreciation of beauty, wonder, mysticism.

Then one further level above self-actualisation:

- Transcendence: helping others to realise their potential.

This hierarchy is dependent upon the lower levels of need being satisfactorily met in order that higher levels can then be achieved. For example, if basic physiological needs are lacking, further development in any of the other areas will be impaired.

> Once each of the needs have been met, if at a future time there is a deficiency in the meeting of a need then the motivation to remove the deficiency will be experienced by the individual.
>
> (Maslow 1954)

How well the foundation building blocks of Maslow's hierarchy had been established for the children participating in Wellie Wednesday was therefore a necessary consideration. In some cases, improvement started to occur only when the intervention began at the most basic first level needs, those dealing with hunger and physical comfort. For this reason, breakfast was provided to start the day and spare warm clothes were kept available if anyone arrived inadequately dressed for outdoor sessions. The fire was at the heart of our area and served as a practical and symbolic centre to our day.

A further analysis of Maslow's hierarchy of needs has been identified by what have been named as the 'human givens', developed by Joe Griffin and Ivan Tyrrell (2007), an approach to emotional health which, at its core, attempts to find and address unmet innate needs common to all humans, termed 'givens'. As mentioned in the previous chapter we used these givens to form the basis of discussions with parents and carers of what gaps in emotional needs there might be for their child.

Emotional needs include:

- Security: feelings of safety and a safe environment in which to live.
- Attention: to give and receive it.
- Sense of autonomy and control: to make responsible choices.
- Emotional intimacy: acceptance.
- Feeling part of a wider community.
- Privacy, opportunity to reflect and consolidate experience.
- Sense of status within social groupings.
- Sense of competence and achievement.
- Meaning and purpose, which come from being stretched in what we do and think.

The resources nature gave us to help us meet our needs include:

- The ability to develop complex long-term memory, which enables us to add to our knowledge and learn.
- The ability to build rapport, empathise and connect with others.

- Imagination, which enables us to focus our attention away from our emotions, to use language and solve problems more creatively and objectively.
- Emotions and instincts.
- A conscious, rational mind that can check out our emotions, question, analyse and plan.
- An observing self: that part of us that can step back, be more objective and be aware of itself.
- A dreaming brain that works to process experiences during sleeping time.

These ideas were explored in group discussions with parents and carers using 'I feel ...' statements and a concentric circle diagram (see Chapter 17) to assess how well each of their child's emotional needs was being met. To help identify the meaning behind each need, an 'I' statement was used. Often, what started as an exploration of children's needs also became of personal relevance to the adults. Adults found themselves recognising their own needs and finding ways to address them. Dialogues also started between children and adults, and changes were made in the homes of families as a result of this exercise.

Security and safeness
- I feel safe when ...

Attention
- Someone who notices me is ...

Emotional connection
- ... are important in my life.

Control and autonomy
- I like being able to ...

Connection to the wider community
- One thing I can do to make my school a better place is ...

Competence and achievement
- Something I feel proud of is ...

Status and acceptance
- ... likes me because ...

Being valued
- I feel special because ...

Privacy
- I like spending time on my own doing ...

Challenge
- Something I did that was difficult was ...

Responsibility
•   Something I can be trusted to do is …

Purpose and belief system
•   One thing I believe is really important is …
•   Something that would make the world a better place is …

The initial and ongoing assessments for individual children before they joined Wellie Wednesday looked for any developmental gaps that would need to be filled in order to enable further progression.

The Boxall profile helped to identify need and monitor progress using pre-, post- and follow-up assessments. From interpreting each child's profile, individual learning targets were set, then activities devised to address them.

The Boxall profile

The Boxall profile was first developed in the 1980s (Bennathon and Boxall 1998) following extensive development work with Nurture Group teachers and teaching assistants. It was developed to provide a more precise way of assessing pupils' needs, planning intervention and measuring progress. It was standardised by the then Inner London Education Authority (ILEA) research and statistics branch and published in 1984. It is now available through the Social, Emotional and Behavioural Difficulties Association (SEBDA). The norms apply to children with 'no problems evident' aged between three years four months and eight years. The Boxall profile consists of two sections, the developmental strand and the diagnostic profile.

The developmental strands

These consist of items that describe different aspects of the developmental process of the pre-school years. Satisfactory completion of this first stage of learning is essential if children are to make good use of their educational opportunities. The statements are clustered into two groups:

Cluster 1: the organisation of experience.
Cluster 2: the internalisation of controls.

A high score on this scale suggests a child is well able to take advantage of the opportunities offered in school.

The diagnostic profile

This consists of items describing behaviour that inhibits or interferes with the child's satisfactory involvement in school. They are directly or indirectly the outcome of impaired learning in the earliest years. The profile has three clusters:

Cluster 1: self-limiting features, identifies children who lack the normal thrust for growth.

Cluster 2: under developed behaviour, identifies features that lack the inner resources to relate to others and engage at an age appropriate level.

Cluster 3: unsupported development, suggests children who have marked negativism towards others, are anti-social, angry, which may be a result of lack of early nurture or intrusive negative experiences.

High scores on the diagnostic profile show a range of difficulties, which would inhibit learning.

The scores are drawn up on a bar chart giving a visual representation of the child's profile. Once a Boxall profile has been completed, to be interpreted fully, the two parts need to be looked at together and attention given to identifying strengths as well as difficulty. Children in need of extra support, for example, a nurture group, generally have relatively low scores on the developmental strands and relatively high scores on a few or many of the clusters in the diagnostic profile.

In addition to the Boxall profiles, each child's parent or carer and class teacher filled in a Strengths and Difficulties Questionnaire. These were useful for collecting anecdotal information during the initial assessment interviews. Class teachers completed a Boxall profile for each child participating in the Wellie Wednesday project; this provided valuable insight into the child as seen by their teacher.

Goodman's Strengths and Difficulties Questionnaire (SDQ)

Goodman's Strengths and Difficulties Questionnaire is a brief behavioural screening questionnaire about 4–16-year-olds. It exists in several versions. All versions of the SDQ ask about 25 attributes, some positive and some negative. These 25 items are divided into five scales:

1. Emotional symptoms (five items).
2. Conduct problems (five items).
3. Hyperactivity/inattention (five items).
4. Peer relationship problems (five items).
5. Pro social behaviour (five items).

The same 25 items are included in questionnaires for completion by the parents or teachers of 4–16-year-olds. SDQs were used in initial interviews before starting on Wellie Wednesday. These provided a useful and positive way of hearing about each child and gaining understanding of the parents' views. It helped to encourage them to acknowledge their child's strengths rather than to focus solely on the difficulties. Teachers also filled in the questionnaires, which provided a valuable overview of the child in school. The views from home and school helped to build a more complete picture of the child.

A solution-focused approach

Solution Focused Brief Therapy has been developed by Steve de Shazer (1985) with ideas taken from family therapy and innovations and ideas from Milton Erickson.

Extensive research evidence has been validated across a range of settings. It provides a method of working with people that:

- Looks at the person not the problem.
- Focuses on personal strengths and qualities.
- Explores possibilities and a preferred future.
- Recognises changes that lead to the preferred future.
- Respects the person as the expert in their own life.

In our educational setting, where there was no attempt at engaging in any form of therapy, the principles of the approach were applicable to both the speaking and listening and emotional literacy elements of sessions with children. It was also a useful approach when working with the parents and carers as it helped them to focus on small things that were working well and use them to plan a positive future.

A solution-focused approach:

- Provided a positive way of dealing with what had previously tended to be problem-centred referrals. It was an appropriate way of engaging positively with parents or carers as well as children.
- Did not require delving into personal situations or problems and was therefore suitable for individual and group work.
- Sees the person as being in control of or responsible for creating change, thereby reducing dependence on outside agencies (O'Hanlon and Weiner-Davis 1998).

During conversations with parent and carers, and in whole group discussions, the importance of being solution-focused was paramount. An awareness that the focus must always be brought back to what works prevents groups from strengthening the emphasis on problems then spiralling into negativity.

The key principles were as follows:

- In order to develop solutions it is not necessary to explore in detail the causes of problems; sometimes it is unhelpful to assume the cause is known.
- There are always times when things are better; these exceptions to the problem provide an insight into what works.
- Big changes can start with small changes.
- Everyone has a contribution to make that is of importance to him or her.
- Everyone has strengths; identifying them empowers the children to become part of the solution.
- Knowing what works means it can be repeated.

Narrative conversations

Narrative approaches, developed by The Dulwich Centre Community Mental Health Project, Adelaide Australia, are an extension of solution-focused brief therapy (Morgan 2000). The aims of narrative conversations are to recognise that:

- Problems are seen as being separate from the person, i.e. 'the problem is the problem'.

- The person has the potential to reduce the influence of the problem on their lives.
- Curiosity and a willingness to ask questions we don't know the answers to lead to meaningful insights for the person.
- There are many directions a conversation can take.
- The person needs to be significantly involved in determining the path to be taken.

When a person experiences a problem they often see it as a reflection of their character, nature and worth. It takes on a dominant story of failure or being to blame. Externalising conversations creates space for the person to separate from the problem that is affecting their life. They are then in a position to take a new course of action, to find an alternative story. They can then resist or protest or renegotiate with the problem in other ways (Epston et al. 1997).

The conversation leads to the problem becoming personified and preferably named, for example, through:

- Exploration of its tactics: Where and when does the problem arise?
- Ways of operating: How does it cause trouble? In what ways?
- Intentions: What is it trying to do? What purpose does the problem serve?
- 'Tricks': How does the problem sneak up on you?
- Likes and dislikes: What helps and what hampers the problem?
- Motives: Why does the problem persist? Why did it start?
- Rules: What does the problem make you do?
- Deceits or lies: What does the problem make you believe?

Once it develops a persona of its own, the relationship between the person and the problem can be explored more fully. This is followed by conversations looking at changing the current relationship between the person and the problem to a future one that suits the person better. Visualising and role-playing different possibilities help to enrich the experience of imagining a successful alternative story. Externalising the problem and using a playful approach to learning more about how to keep Trouble out or outwit Trouble, helps to reduce anxiety and enhance belief in the possibility of 'change for the better' happening.

Examples of where this was helpful to individual children include:

- Keeping 'Rush and Guess' out of maths.
- Keeping 'Trouble' out of the playground.
- Letting 'Truthful Honesty' help with telling the truth.
- Keeping 'Crossness' out.

Joe said:

> It was too noisy, the door was open and let 'Crossness' in. 'Crossness' is like a big ghost. He makes me really cross. He smiles with all his mouths. He thinks it's funny when I get cross. I am going to win. When 'Crossness' is gone you'll see a happy Joe. He can do good ignoring.

'Crossness' has gone now ... I think he's gone on holiday with his family. He couldn't win me anymore. I might have killed him right under the ground. If I felt him coming I keep him in until I get out in the playground and go to the grass and do karate kicks.

Promoting alternative thinking skills: PATHS

The PATHS programme, developed by Mark Greenberg and Carol Kusche (1994), is a whole school curriculum that has been shown to significantly improve children's social and emotional skills. Social emotional competence underlies effective behaviour and academic success. The PATHS programme provides a systematic developmental approach for enhancing social and emotional understanding and academic competence in children. Whilst unsuitable for following as a curriculum in a short-term project, the background knowledge derived from previously delivering the materials in schools enabled Wellie Wednesday to utilise some of PATHS core messages. The programme covers five domains of social and emotional development:

- Self-control.
- Emotional understanding.
- Positive self-esteem.
- Relationships.
- Interpersonal problem-solving skills.

Its aims include:

- To establish and reinforce basic classroom rules.
- To strengthen self-control and encourage reflective thinking.
- To improve children's communication skills.
- To increase children's abilities to identify, understand and discuss the variety of feelings people experience in their daily lives.
- To enhance children's abilities to recognise and interpret similarities and differences in the feelings, reactions and points of view in themselves and others.
- To promote the development of empathy and perspective-taking.
- To help children use problem-solving skills to prevent or resolve problems and conflicts in social interactions.

Wellie Wednesday focused upon the five domains of social and emotional development; these contributed to the core foundation of the programme that was developed.

Sensory development

When assessing cognitive levels of development, attention was also paid to the sensory developmental stages. These are required in order to facilitate the necessary integration for successful learning to take place. Even before birth, the senses are stimulated to feed information back to the brain. After birth, there is a natural progression through gross and fine motor development, followed by increasing perceptual awareness. Only then can the cognitive skills fully develop. Figure 18.1 has been adapted from the sensory

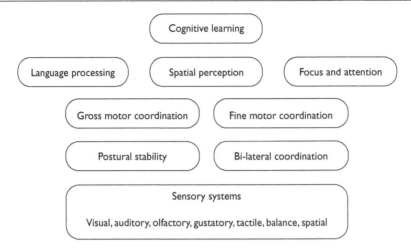

Figure 18.1 Sensory integration hierarchy.

Source: Adapted from Taylor and Trott 1991.

integration pyramid created by Kathleen Taylor and Maryann Trott (1991), which can be used to assess any areas of weakness. At the lower levels, weaknesses could be impairing learning in school. Inattention, fidgeting and poor literacy skills were often referral concerns. Seen as symptoms rather than behavioural traits, they could be used as indicators of stages of sensory integration that had not been successfully achieved.

The Wellie Wednesday programme incorporated sensory development opportunities as 'second chance learning' (Winnicott 1982). A range of exercises and activities were offered that developed coordination and perceptual skills normally acquired at a younger age. Gross motor activities included balancing and crossing the body's mid line. Fine motor activities included making mini environments, creating small worlds in sand trays, weaving and braiding. Practising stillness was a vital part of children being in control of their own bodies; this enabled them to better observe and use their senses to explore the world around them.

Vygotsky's zone of proximal development

Lev Vygotsky (1896–1934) was a psychologist whose main work was in developmental psychology. He proposed a theory that the development of cognitive functions leads to the emergence of reasoning, which needs to be experienced in a social environment.

> What a child can perform today with assistance s/he will be able to perform tomorrow independently.
>
> (Lev Vygotsky)

He proposed that the zone of proximal development is the distance between the *actual* developmental level, as determined by independent problem-solving, and the level of *potential* development as determined through problem-solving under adult guidance ('scaffolding'), or in collaboration with more capable peers.

What children can do with the assistance of others is even more indicative of their mental development than what they can do alone.

(Lev Vygotsky)

- The zone of proximal development (ZPD) has been described as the 'buds' of developing competence rather than the fruit of actual development.
- The ZPD embodies a concept of readiness to learn that emphasises upper levels of competence. These upper boundaries are not absolute, but are constantly extending with the learner's increasing independent competence.
- The actual developmental level characterises cognitive development retrospectively, whilst the zone of proximal development characterises cognitive development predictively.
- Human learning presupposes a specific social nature and is part of a process by which children grow into the intellectual life of those around them.
- An essential feature of learning is that it awakens a variety of internal developmental processes that are able to operate only when the child is interacting with people in their environment and in cooperation with peers.

Scaffolding requires the teacher to support pupils, whilst providing them with the opportunity to extend their current skills and knowledge, by enabling them to access learning that independently they would be unable to attempt. According to Vygotsky the teacher does this by:

- Engaging the students' interest.
- Simplifying tasks so that they are manageable.
- Motivating students to pursue the given task.

In addition, the teacher must:

- Look for discrepancies between students' efforts and the solution.
- Control frustration and risk.
- Model approaches to successful task completion (Hausfather 1996).

Vygotsky's findings inspired and motivated our belief in potential and the importance of social connectedness in learning and development. At Wellie Wednesday every child was seen as having the potential to succeed within the supportive environment.

Instrumental enrichment programme and mediated learning experience

Reuven Feuerstein (1921–2014) conducted studies which led him to believe in structural cognitive modifiability by means of what he identifies as the mediated learning experience (MLE). This occurs naturally between parent and offspring but is also the means by which cognitive dysfunctions can be successfully remediated. This is analogous to Vygotsky's scaffolding in that it requires the teacher to invest greater meaning into the learning response, i.e. to insert human interpretation into the process thereby incorporating a powerful additional dimension to learning.

Having identified the strategies used by successful learners he devised a programme known as Instrumental Enrichment (IE) to teach the necessary cognitive skills to those who have not acquired them through the normal developmental and educational means (Feuerstein et al. 1980).

> Everyone can learn, can change.
>   The child is not deficient in the ability to learn but rather has not had sufficient mediated learning experiences to develop the cognitive processes.
>
> (Reuven Feuerstein)

Feuerstein's studies led him to believe that:

- Certain cognitive functions were essential in order to be able to organise and retain experiences and thus to learn from them. Without these functions in place, individuals remain either passive or impulsive when confronted with new learning.
- Impaired thinking skills impact upon social and behavioural as well as academic progress.
- Cognitive dysfunctions can always be modified.
- Cognitive skills, once in place, set off self-generating improvement so post-intervention cognitive improvements are likely to continue.

At Wellie Wednesday, an awareness of the cognitive functions and how to develop them through mediated interactions of speaking, listening and problem-solving activities, enabled children to move from passivity or impulsivity to active engagement and more reflective thinking.

To be *successful learners* we need to:

- Explore systematically what we have to do.
  Missing out some of the instructions or information leads to mistakes.
- Understand the words and ideas being used.
  Learn new vocabulary.
- Understand the concepts of size, distance or position.
  Spatial awareness.
- Use more than one type of information.
  e.g., *Work with shape and size.*
- Define the task.
  Know exactly what it is you have to do.
- Use information stored in the brain.
  Memory or visual transport.
- Make comparisons.
  Look for similarities to and differences from what you already know.
- Use what is relevant.
  Look for the details that apply to the task.
- Summarise information.
  Put into your own words what you have learnt.
- Use planning to avoid guess work.
  'Think before you do.'

- Express your thoughts and control your actions.
  Using 'not OK' behaviour does not solve problems.
- Use words and concepts accurately to avoid mistakes.
  Explain what you are thinking or feeling.
- Communicate so that others know what you mean.
  Put yourself in the other person's position. Will they be able to understand what you mean?

(Adapted from Feuerstein et al (1999))

The more these cognitive functions are developed the better the thinking will be, thereby leading to improved learning and social interaction.

Vygotsky and Feuerstein's theories provided an optimistic expectation that we would see change and progress. This was fundamental to our core belief when devising our curriculum. Children were better able to attempt new ways of thinking within a supportive social setting, an environment that fostered curiosity and awakened interest through carefully mediated learning challenges.

Attachment-focused family therapy

As educationalists, our role was not to offer therapy but to feel secure in the knowledge that our ways of working would not exacerbate any emotional difficulties a child might be suffering, especially for those who had experienced trauma. The work of Daniel Hughes (2006, 2007) provided clear guidelines as to how foster parents were trained to work, along with insights into how therapists would aim to bring about change. These approaches were very much in line with the ways of working we had developed for Wellie Wednesday and gave us further confidence and greater knowledge on which to build. The following extracts were adapted from Daniel Hughes' guidelines for attachment-based family-focused therapy. They are the features that we incorporated to build firm foundations into our education based programme. We recognised that ideally children needed to share the whole experience with their parent or carer. As Daniel Hughes explains:

> For the purpose of increasing the child's psychological safety, his readiness to rely on significant attachment figures in his life, and his ability to resolve and integrate the dysregulating experiences a person who is a primary attachment figure to the child will be actively present.

Wellie Wednesday sessions were grounded in playfulness, acceptance, curiosity, and empathy (PACE). The team aimed to support the parents and carers in further developing their relationship through drawing on 'PLACE' in their interactions. PLACE requires an attachment figure to be:

- Playful
- Loving
- Accepting
- Curious
- Empathic

By acknowledging love in their relationship, the parent or carer was clearly identifiable as the attachment figure. Support from the team was aiming to enhance this relationship thus further strengthening the bonds of attachment. The attachment figure role is to:

- Help the child to feel safe.
- Communicate PLACE both non-verbally and verbally.
- Help the child to regulate any negative effect, such as fear, shame, anger or sadness.
- Validate the child's worth.
- Provide attachment security.
- Help the child to make sense of their life so that it is organised and congruent.
- Help the child to understand the parent's or carer's perspective and intentions towards them.

In addition, the guidelines aim to facilitate effective discipline whilst reducing feelings of shame and developing skills. Knowing these guidelines gave us confidence that the way in which we worked was based in sound theoretical background. Daniel Hughes' discipline guidelines include:

1. Stay physically close.
2. Make choices for the child and structure activities.
3. Set and maintain your favoured emotional tone, not the child's.
4. Accept thoughts, feelings, wishes, intentions and perceptions of the child.
5. Provide natural and logical consequences for behaviour.
6. Be predictable in your attitude, less predictable in your consequences.
7. Re-attune following an experience of resistance.
8. Convey with empathy that you are not overwhelmed by the child's behaviour.
9. Use the child's anger to build a stronger connection.
10. Ensure that there is reciprocal communication of thoughts and feelings.
11. Be directive and firm, but also be attuned to the emotional state of the child.
12. Be proactive in reducing the child's ability to hurt you or others, either physically or emotionally.

It was notable that trust was deepened when points 7 and 9 were explained to key workers in schools and they were able to follow a child's angry outburst by staying physically and emotionally available to them. By reassuringly helping them to de-escalate, the child began to look for support and accept guidance at times of frustration or anxiety, thus reducing the need for outbursts.

How the brain responds to kindness and safety

At the core of the project was the belief that kindness and safety are two vital elements in promoting the development of a satisfactorily functioning emotional system, which in turn allows for good cognitive development.

Paul Gilbert (2009; see also Porges 2007) explains that humans have evolved three systems that regulate emotion. These systems work differently but interact in complex ways. Understanding them can provide insight into what may be useful in devising ways of working with children who struggle with managing their feelings and behaviour.

- **Incentive- and resource-focused system:** excites, gives drive and motivates. When balanced by the other two systems this one enables goal setting and energising pleasure seeking. Over stimulation leads to frustration and disappointment when winning and wanting something cannot always be achieved.
- **Threat-focused system:** activated to seek safety from anger, disgust and anxiety. It is engaged when danger is perceived. In an activated state, attention is given only to cues about danger and safety. The senses are scanning for threats whilst overriding and disengaging the system that connects to others. It even reduces the ability to hear or interpret what others are saying. Children in chronic threat-focused mode are going to struggle in school, socially and academically.
- **Affiliative-focused system:** seeks soothing through connectedness, safeness and feelings of contentment. This newest system activates when we understand that we are in a safe environment. When it's switched on, we have the capacity to be socially engaged, to think, to hear and understand other humans, to eat, to play and feel content.

Whilst physical survival is facilitated by the first two systems, the third system is stimulated to develop by the experiences of the child in relation to its caregivers. Firstly, physical affection is experienced in highly sensory ways through touch, facial expression, being held and comforted. Secondly, as needs are met, and soothing and comfort feelings are experienced, the child learns to trust and realises that they exist independently but are 'held in mind' by others. As these experiences are laid down as memories, the child learns to think of others as kind and supportive, and themselves as lovable. The resulting feelings are of safeness and contentment. Children also learn to recognise feelings of approval and disapproval and how to elicit them, enabling them to start to understand social interactions. As they interact, they are able to experience the joy and fun of being with others. Activation of the soothing system releases chemical signals that as well as having the feel-good factor are also received by the threat system, allowing it to remain inactive.

Children who have been less fortunate have not had sufficient experiences to develop the parts of the brain required for kindness and empathy. They tend to be ever alert for threats, real or perceived. Feelings of anxiety are designed to keep the body and mind alert and primed for fight, flight or freeze reactions and these can all serve well as survival mechanisms. When activated the system produces high levels of a stress hormone, cortisol, but this will also serve as a primer for using the defensive emotion of aggression. This would have been useful in genuinely dangerous states, such as our early ancestors may have experienced. Designed for short bursts of survival reactions, if this system is activated into a chronic state of anxiety it is not only unpleasant to experience but damaging in the long term. Children who experience this highly reactive state may be seen in school as being very angry or one of those who flee. Less noticed, but just as in need of help, are those who freeze, hearing little, learning even less and remaining socially withdrawn or isolated. The high arousal anxiety state potentially impairs brain development, especially the frontal and pre-frontal cortex areas, which are required for higher-level thinking, reasoning and problem-solving. These are the very areas that are required to be in full use in learning situations.

If a child is to reach their learning potential in school and cope, they will need to be able to function, not only in the academic learning environment, but also within its social setting. A supportive and enriching environment that can offer nurturing experiences will give second chance developmental opportunities.

Wellie Wednesday offered safeness (including clear boundaries), kindness, caring, nurturing (through food, physical warmth and playfulness) and emotional warmth (making explicit that children, parents and carers were valued members of the group). As the human brain is primed for responding to kindness and safety, children were usually quick to respond to the way words were used to reassure and affirm. Even during challenging times, an adult calmly stating that the need was to keep themselves and others safe, would help to de-escalate a situation. The team were careful to consider their tone of voice and body language at all times but especially at these more challenging times. Reminders were given to the children, and adults, that being kind to themselves and keeping themselves safe was very important. This was an explicit addition to the school expectation of using safe behaviour towards others and being kind to others.

Schools also found this awareness helpful and were able to change their responses when they could see disruptive and aggressive behaviour as being anxiety-driven. The teacher using words to reassure changed one child's frequent running out of class and school. As his behaviour escalated, she would say: 'It is my job as the adult to keep you safe so I need to know where you are.' If he bolted for the door she would say: 'Remember to stay where I can see you so that I know you are safe.' At first he would still leave his seat but he would hover at the classroom door instead of running down the corridor and trying to get outside. As his trust in his teacher grew, he had less need to run.

Another highly reactive child was helped by being offered a safe place with a cushion tucked in beside a filing cabinet near the teacher's desk. He was told: 'I care about you so I need to keep you safe and near me when you feel upset.'

Where it all began: Some background information

Primary Behaviour and Attendance Strategy Pilot: Small group work for vulnerable children and their parents (2004)

Wellie Wednesday was based on previous small group and parenting projects undertaken in schools and during sessions at a pupil referral unit. For insight into the forerunners of the project, the following text is taken from a full report of a small group work pilot study. Fourteen small groups were run in four schools; 53 pupils participated.

The dynamics of various sized groups had previously been trialled, showing that the aim of the group was key to determining its size.

- More than six members required a class delivery style, as listening skills and concentration are stretched too far if everyone was given a say in response to questions.
- Where delivery of the PATHS curriculum was required, a larger group of fourteen was appropriate as this required the skill of listening in a larger group.
- A longer session directed at improving thinking skills targeted six pupils at a time.

- Children who needed to develop social and behavioural skills and those who needed to improve their speech, language and concentration skills required a smaller group size of four. Smaller numbers were crucial to being able to pick up on the detail of each child's thinking and language.

The presenting needs of the referred children were identified as:

- Aggression.
- Impulsivity.
- Lack of empathy.
- Disruptive behaviour.
- Anxiety.
- Passivity or lack of engagement with learning.
- Poor language skills.
- Negativity towards self or others.

Eight groups incorporated:

- Basic social skills.
- Positive behaviour targets.
- Impulsivity control.

Two groups concentrated on:

- Improving listening skills.
- Developing thinking skills.
- Raising expectations.

One group (children who had experienced trauma in their past) addressed:

- Developing self-worth and positive self-image.
- Exploring change and hope.
- Seeing things from different viewpoints.
- Coping strategies and strengths.

Two groups focused on:

- Self-control.
- Feelings.
- Relationships.

One group required:

- Cooperative working.
- Establishing routines and boundaries.
- Gross and fine motor control skills.

Key principles of the group work

- Establishing relationships that were warm and affirming was a priority.
- Children were helped to see themselves as valued members of the group.
- Shared cooperative activities and a strong emphasis on talking and listening encouraged group identity and feeling valued.
- Ways of doing things were discussed with the children, who were made aware of the consequences of behavioural choices.
- Feelings and behaviour were talked about.
- Children were helped to recognise that they felt more positive when they joined in constructively.
- The principle of positive reinforcement was paramount.

It is well recognised that children will gain attention through their behaviour. Adults can either notice and comment on what they like a child to do, or notice and comment on what the child is getting wrong. When adults comment on a child's behaviour it is reinforced, making it easier for the child to do it again. It is therefore possible to influence whether a child develops negative or positive behaviour. To follow this principle, low-level off task behaviour had to be ignored. Within a small group this can be hard to achieve, particularly if the child escalates the behaviour. A whole group target tick chart was used to give immediate praise to the other children for things they were getting right, for example, good sitting, good listening, or indeed good ignoring, which trained pupils to ignore another's off task behaviour through gaining praise themselves (the alternative being to join in, as often happens when the behaviour attracts comment from the teacher). Usually, being ignored was sufficient to curb the off task behaviour. As soon as an attempt at getting it right was made, the teacher gave the child praise (Webster Stratton 1980–2011).

Cooperative learning was at the core of every session in accordance with Vygotsky's social construction of knowledge theory. Research (Jenkins and O'Connor 2003) showed that children are introduced to new thought patterns and understanding through dialogue with peers. For this reason, groups of children of mixed verbal and intellectual ability were preferable. This enabled less articulate children to gain greater exposure to their peers' extended use of language.

Discussion was part of every activity. Reflection on how tasks had been successfully completed and any improvements that could have been made followed each task. Group identity (naming of each group, for example, Tuesday group) was also reinforced through talking about successful whole group participation and completion of each task (Johnson and Johnson 1994).

Resource interdependence (Putnam 1998) was an initial key to developing group cohesion and establishing cooperation rather than competition. Cooperative games were used to start the sessions, for example, each member was given a part of a train track that needed to be constructed out of ten interlocking pieces, finishing it without using all the parts had to be avoided or the train would not run. Children needed to be aware of each other's pieces and allow others a turn first if they held the final piece. Group scores to beat their own record were also used with games to restrain impulsivity, for example, balancing games such as One Too Many (Waddingtons) and Penguin Pile Up (Ravensburger).

A group target tick chart was used to positively reward social skills of sharing, helping, encouraging, listening. The chart acted as reinforcement initially. Subsequently, although it remained a prop, as little attention as possible was paid to the overall score once the system had become established. This fading out of the extrinsic reward was an important aim. The need was for children to recognise and then to actively seek the intrinsic rewards of:

• Feeling better about themselves.
• Developing pride in their work.
• Gaining pleasure in peer relationships.
• Satisfaction in task completion.
• Cooperating with adults and peers.

If the focus is on the extrinsic reward to be given at the end of the session, these real benefits can fail to be valued or even noticed. A sticker may occasionally be used as a very temporary first step (for example, if the children were used to receiving stickers) whilst weaning them onto the intrinsic reward system. Extrinsic reward systems run the risk of being given in order to avoid disappointment or to encourage even when not truly deserved. Unexpected stickers or stamps given after work is completed can be used randomly to reinforce effort and enjoyment.

Sometimes giving a sticker to a child before they start work on the understanding that it is theirs to keep as long as they complete the task can be helpful where a child does not really believe they are capable of earning a reward. Parents and carers were taught to use temporary stickers, stars or smiley face charts in order to develop a specific behaviour, for example, for staying in bed. The adults had to first understand the principle that sticker charts will only work if the reward of parental praise or warmth is also present.

Empathy building and developing the ability to see things from another point of view were key themes to be returned to. Speaking and listening times were incorporated into every session. Children asked each other questions about their contributions. Solutions were sought from the group for any problems that may have been experienced by an individual. Through the experience of being listened to, these face-to-face interactions increased self-respect and feelings of empathy for the speaker and the 'adviser' child. Initially the modelling of these roles by the two adults was important. The adults verbalised dilemmas, difficulties and mistakes, then following a suggestion, demonstrated how to cope with mistake making and how to give and receive help.

The phrase 'check and change' (adapted from Lake and Needham 1995) was used to praise individuals when they dealt with being wrong positively. Learning that it is acceptable to find you were wrong (learning by your mistakes) requires flexibility in thinking, i.e. the ability to reassess decisions as new information is acquired. Check and change is a vital building block in the foundations of good thinking, required for academic success and for addressing behavioural and social issues.

Self-efficacy is the perception of one's capabilities to carry out and meet the demands of situations (Bandura 1998). It influences levels of motivation, mastery of experiences, thought patterns and emotional reactions to situations. To enhance self-efficacy:

• Mastery of skills was demonstrated in a number of ways, for example, through the use of simple exercises such as balance boards, koosh ball catch. These clearly demonstrated to children that what they could not do initially, with practice and support they became able to do independently ('scaffolding').

• Role modelling: seeing how their peers practised something.
• Rehearsing a situation so they can develop the skills they will require, for example, for a shy or language-impaired child practising asking a question before being sent to another adult on an errand.
• Role-playing alternative endings to a situation.
• Self-control through use of stress relief techniques, using relaxation and controlled breathing and music to practise feeling calm. Linking self-control to calming down high arousal states of anger and upset by using calming down strategies. Progress was recognised through the mediation of challenge, (see Feuerstein et al. 1999). Both group challenges and more specific individual challenges were identified. Challenges were linked to:
  – Externalising of a problem (see Chapter 10), for example, 'To notice some times when "Little Voice" didn't stop you speaking up.' (For a child who was withdrawn and non-verbal in school but had identified that although at school she had 'little voice' at home she had 'loud voice'.)
  – Defeatism: using the 'I can't YET' challenge gets the brain ready for being able to do it soon.
  – Overcoming distress at apparent failure, for example, when a ball is dropped or a balancing game falls.
  – Eliminating low-level disruption, teaching the children vigilance to watch out for their own impulsivity, for example, 'The pencil is tempting you to pick it up and start before you know what to do.' Children would struggle not to be tricked.
  – Lack of confidence (Seligman 2006).

Small first steps were designed, which, when successful, led to the next slightly harder challenge. For example, a self-conscious child initially did not want to leave the table to take part in action rhymes. His first step was to just stand alongside the group but with no further requirement to join in. Step two was to add the actions and step three was to say the words with the group. A final step was to follow his peers' example of doing it independently. The 'stepped' challenge achieved the same end without resulting in upset or entrenched refusal. When a large stride is too big no amount of cajoling or pressure will make it possible, but if small steps cover the distance then the same place can be reached. The next time the stride may not seem so big. The role of the group work was to create small steps until greater strides could be taken.

Reflection

How can developing a theoretical background to our work inform our everyday practice?

References

Bennathan, M. and Boxall, M. (1998). *The Boxall profile: a guide to effective intervention in the education of pupils with emotional and behavioural difficulties: Handbook for teachers.*

Nurture Group Consortium; Association of Workers for Children with Emotional and Behavioural Difficulties. Maidstone: AWCEBD.

De Shazer, S. (1985). *Key to solutions in brief therapy*. New York: W.W. Norton and Company.

Epston, D., Freeman, M. and Lobovotis, D. (1997). Playful approaches to serious problems: Narrative therapy with children and their families. New York: Norton.

Feuerstein, R., Rand, Y, Hoffman, M.B. and Miller, R. (1980). *Instrumental enrichment: An intervention program for cognitive modifiability*. Baltimore: University Park Press.

Gilbert, P. (2009). *The compassionate mind: A new approach to life's challenges*. Oakland, California: New Harbinger Publications.

Greenberg, M. and Kusche, C. (1995). *Promoting alternative thinking strategies (PATHS)*. South Deerfield: Channing Bete.

Griffin, A. and Tyrrell, I. (2007). *An idea in practice: Using the human givens approach*. Hailsham: Human Givens Publishing Ltd.

Hausfather, S. (1996). Vygotsky and schooling: Creating a social context for learning. *Action in Teacher Education*. London: Taylor & Francis.

Hughes, D. (2006). *Building the bonds of attachment*. New York: Jason Aronson Inc.

Hughes, D. (2007). *Attachment focused family therapy*. New York: W.W. Norton and Company.

Maslow, A.H. (1954). *Motivation and personality*. New York: Harper.

Morgan, A. (2000). *What is narrative therapy?: An easy to read introduction*. Adelaide: Dulwich Centre Publications.

O'Hanlon, W. and Weiner-Davis, M. (1998). *In search of solutions*. New York: W.W. Norton and Company.

Porges, S.W. (2007). *The polyvagal theory: Neurophysical foundations of emotions, attachment communications and self regulation*. NewYork: W.W. Norton and Company.

Taylor, K. and Trott, M. (1991). Sensory learning pyramid, adapted from Autism Central Pty Ltd.

Background information section

Bandura, A. (1998). *Self-efficacy: The exercise of control*. New York: W.H. Freeman.

Feuerstein, R., Klein, P.S. and Tannenbaum, A.J. (1999). Mediated learning experience. Tel Aviv: Freund Publishing House.

Jenkins, J.R. and O'Connor, R.E. (2003). *Handbook of learning disabilities*. New York: Guilford.

Johnson, D.W. and Johnson, R.T. (1994). *Learning together and alone: Cooperative, competitive and individualistic learning*. Boston: Allyn & Bacon.

Lake, M. and Needham, M. (1995). *Top ten thinking tactics: A practical introduction to the thinking skills revolution*. Birmingham: Imaginative Minds.

Putnam, J. (1998). *Co-operative learning and strategies for inclusion*. London: Brookes.

Seligman, M. (1991, revised edition 2006). *Learned optimism: How to change your mind and your life*. New York:Vintage Books.

Webster Stratton, C. (1980–2011). The Incredible Years Parents, Teachers, and Children Training Series: Program content, methods, research and dissemination. Seattle, USA: Incredible Years.

Conclusion

Transferring learning into school and some final thoughts

> There are two lasting bequests we can hope to give our children. One of these is roots, the other, wings.
>
> (Hodding Carter)

The aim of this book is to provide a resource for practitioners who work with children who have a high level of social and emotional need, and whose behaviour is subsequently challenging. The strategies described here may be used to create programmes specific to an individual child's needs and the setting in which they are working.

The underpinning principle of the Wellie Wednesday project is based upon the belief that children with challenging behaviour may fail to access the school curriculum successfully because of their unmet needs, either emotionally, developmentally or cognitively. The Wellie Wednesday approach used to address children's needs continues to develop as some of the original team members begin to establish their own programmes, using and extending the ideas within their outdoor provision and in school.

The strategies described here can, to a certain extent, be successful within an indoor school setting as they were developed from small group work in schools (see Chapter 18). However, in the Wellie Wednesday project, the outdoor countryside setting provided an even more effective vehicle for learning, and in some cases unlearning, unravelling old patterns, that needed to take place. Sitting and talking around an open fire and cooking meals was central to creating comfort and a positive group identity. By being in an unfamiliar environment it was possible to leave any negative experiences behind and offer a fresh start for children, parents, carers and schools in their journey to a positive future. It was made clear that 'this is the way it is here'. Children and adults were able to be different 'in this space'.

Every stage of the project was carefully thought out in order to ensure that the children were developing the skills they needed to become competent learners. Firstly, it was recognised that the selected children needed emotional support, that no learning or change could take place if they were emotionally flooded, where anxiety and worries had taken over. This meant that the child had to be accompanied by a parent or carer, that each child had a safe personal space (their tent) and that soothing toys were within reach in times of stress.

Secondly, the parents or carers needed to be receptive to what was being offered and believe that this was a positive way forward for them. The meetings with them before the sessions started ensured that they understood, participated in and embraced the process. When adults responded enthusiastically, change began to happen.

Thirdly, once children were responsive to new ideas and improved their inclination to learn, they began to demonstrate that they could develop skills, knowledge and abilities and their true potential began to evolve. As their strengths were noticed, what was special about each child was nurtured and they were able to flourish. At this stage, carefully chosen activities enabled children to further develop their thinking skills; emphasis was not so much about learning facts, but about developing a new and positive approach to learning. Children were observed closely to establish what they needed to enable them to think clearly and to learn:

• Some were good thinkers but this had not always been evident in tasks they had been set in school.
• Some had the ability to memorise and articulate but had difficulty using this information.
• Some had difficulty processing information.
• Some could process information but not articulate clearly enough to demonstrate their understanding.

When the area of difficulty was understood we were able to design exercises to strengthen that area. For example, Shaun (see Chapter 9) was encouraged to 'think before I do', i.e. take more time processing information before springing into action.

Children were encouraged to see themselves as successful thinkers and learners who were making positive and valued contributions to the group. All contributions were valued within a climate of non-threatening participation. Gradually, the children were able to use their thinking skills to adjust impulsive and inappropriate behaviour that had led to negative outcomes in the past. The negative cycle was broken by defining 'how it is going to be here, in this place, at this time'. Specifically:

• Establishing safe and secure boundaries, respect and trust for each other within the group.
• The use of compliments, everyone noticing the smallest things that each person was getting right, always focusing on the positive.
• Recognition of a positive self, feeling liked and valued and transferring this positive self back into school and home, giving compliments to themselves.
• Opportunities to practise getting it right, resulting in increased confidence in themselves and their abilities.
• Developing a strong group identity where it was believed that everyone could make a positive contribution, an ethos that promoted feelings of acceptance.
• Offering a positive way forward where mistakes give clues about how not to do it next time.
• Schools recognising change and supporting children to apply their learning and make progress back in school (see Introduction).

Over the six weeks of the project a careful progression was planned from an easy start to managing challenge. By the end of six weeks, children were capable of more complicated activities, for instance, they could be trusted to safely use hammers and nails and were taken on an expedition along a disused railway line.

Transferring learning into school

It was of vital importance that the opportunities families had experienced at Wellie Wednesday did not remain isolated episodes but transformed their thinking about life at home and in school. Children were referred from a number of different schools and it was our aim to provide a suggested approach as to how each pupil was going to build upon their success in the project and transfer their progress into the school environment. This was done in a variety of ways, depending on the needs of each child.

- The school identified a person who would meet the child each Thursday to talk about what they had done on the Wednesday, to hear good news, to see anything they had returned with and to help them think how they were going to 'get it right' again today.
- In some cases the child's class teacher or teaching assistant visited the project to ensure that the Wellie Wednesday team and the school were in touch and working together. Seeing the activities in action and their pupil in a different setting created a positive bond between them to build on back in school.
- Pupils were encouraged to talk about their previous day's activities to the rest of the class. In one case, where a child attended a Nurture Group in school he took back ideas (for example, the Wellie Wednesday songs) that his teacher incorporated into her class teaching. Further links were forged with a Wellie Wednesday team member going into the Nurture Group to read carefully selected stories to the group.
- One headteacher regarded a very shy child's participation as important and was pleased and excited when she chose to talk about what she had experienced at Wellie Wednesday. This communicated to the child that her views were valued and gave her the confidence to share her Wellie Wednesday memories with the whole school in an assembly.
- Schools were asked to encourage the children to bring their Wellie Wednesday memories books into school to trigger memory and discussion of their experiences and learning.
- One school set up a special safe place for a child with soothing transitional objects from Wellie Wednesday; holding these provided an alternative to running out of the classroom or becoming destructive.
- Another child was encouraged by the school to keep her Wellie Wednesday puppy shaped bag on her peg. When she became anxious there was an arrangement that she could collect her puppy. Bringing it into the classroom and hanging it on the back of her chair allowed her the time she needed to feel calm again, defusing the situation.
- One school took up the suggestion of a daily ten-minute outdoor session of exercises for a particular child; this helped to continue to improve his coordination and to reduce his fidgeting and inattention.
- A team member was asked to lead a special staff meeting in one school to help build an understanding of how attachment experiences impact on learning and to explore how best to support the adopted child, who was transferring to their school.

- When a child transferred to a new school after attending Wellie Wednesday, the class teacher incorporated many of the ideas into how she organised her class so that it would seem familiar to him. She felt these were beneficial ways of working for all the children (see Chapter 5).
- A team member made visits to school to spend time with each pupil. This was a crucial part of the six-week process. These visits took place after two or three weeks, by which time the children were fully immersed in the new ways of working. The school visits gave an opportunity to explore with each child their good news and how they were making changes at school (see Chapter 10). Meetings with the class teacher also took place. Schools valued these meetings enough to be willing to cover whilst the teacher was out of class. The support that teachers found most useful was being able to consider:
  - Behaviour as a means of communication (i.e. challenging behaviour might be communicating how the child was feeling and explain why a child might behave in a particlar way).
  - How early trauma and attachment styles impact on learning.
  - Practical strategies to address individual needs.
  - Going the extra mile with a vulnerable child.

Long-term change

The school visits continued after the attendance at Wellie Wednesday finished. The frequency of the visits varied; for some it was weekly for a while, for others it was once each half term and in later years once a term. Teachers were free to phone for ongoing support or to arrange an additional visit each if the need arose, for example, sometimes at a later stage a life event, loss, bereavement or violence in the home resulted in fear, anxiety, anger or distress, and caused challenging behaviour to arise again in school. A visit by a team member often helped to reassurethe children and schools through difficult times.

There were many examples of good practice that were truly heartening as headteachers, class teachers and teaching assistants were determined to give a child opportunities for second chance learning. These schools were willing to find ways of dealing sensitively with challenging and often disruptive behaviour in order to avoid the rejection that an exclusion would inevitably have caused. In a few cases, a managed move to a new school was needed to provide a positive way forward.

It was clear that the fundamental values and philosophy of the Wellie Wednesday programme had been taken to heart by many of the academic staff, inspiring them to find creative and sensitive ways to help children deal with challenges and move into a positive future. There were fundamental ways in which the children changed as well. They had gained new ways of thinking, better ways to communicate their feelings and a clearer understanding of others that enabled them to interact and connect more positively.

Evidence of change

Positive comments were received from school staff, including:

Yasmin is a changed child, she used to be a non-participator now she initiates conversation and ideas.

Wellie Wednesday's strength was that it travelled with the children through the year groups.

It has given the children confidence and helps them interact.

Strategies I have used from Wellie Wednesday included empty speech bubble, wait and see, check and change.

Wellie Wednesday has helped children to have more confidence in their school work and feel proud of what they achieve.

The following comments were made by adult participants:

I will always remember the awe and wonder of it all, the special things we shared and the children's excitement.

I will always remember the proud smiles of the children as they talked to the group about their good news and successes.

I will always remember how excited the children became when they achieved something they had struggled with.

The following are words from the children:

Everybody deserves kindness. People who have a lot of kindness have some to give away.

I'm more helpful, really helpful and kind at school. At Wellie Wednesday I noticed more that people liked me.

My hands are kind hands now. I feel excited that I am not hurting anyone, the feelings have gone.

Smiling is good because people smile back at you.

I used to get a good idea and have to say it. Now I know good waiting. I can keep it in until the other person stops the conversation.

I haven't called Mum an idiot for ages … I say I love you.

Trouble all my lifetime makes me get upset. I'm trying not to give him attention. He turned into major trouble. Now I'm trying to help him shrink and be good and turn into Goody.

Thinking helpful thoughts can shrink worried thoughts.

Worry makes me tired out. I shrunk worry by thinking being tired doesn't matter.

I think 'It's OK to wait' when it's not my turn.

I'm more cleverer, really, really clever. Wellie Wednesday makes me happy, makes me do good work.

Being safe that is the whole thing of being alive.

In school, Wellie Wednesday helps me very much, very much I think about it. I do very very concentrating and good looking.

I didn't want to do my work then Miss L. said I could take it to Wellie Wednesday so I did it and asked to stay in at playtime to finish it. I couldn't start my literacy about adjectives. Then Miss L said think about Wellie Wednesday. Then I wrote this. (She showed her page of descriptive writing.)

I use my 'night friends' pillow case as a blanket, then I go straight to sleep without nightmares.

I like the 'see someone special' page in my Wellie Wednesday memories book. (A page with a mirror on it)

Sometimes my strong feelings make other people feel sad. In my heart sometimes I have 'don't want to' feelings, they make me feel angry. (Y used a sign, moving his hand over his heart then up to his head to remind him to move his strong feeling to his thinking brain. As he did it his worried face changed to smiling).

Last week I did feel sad and yesterday I couldn't do my handwriting. I took a little doll from my friend. I thought I should have given it back. I gave it back because I thought I should give it back. 'Change for the better' ... hitting, nipping, punching, taking things are hurting hands, now I think 'keep your hands to yourself', they are kind hands.

The children's comments remind us of their individual characters, the importance of celebrating their strengths and what is special about every one of them.

At last someone understands how it feels and seems to be me without wanting to analyse me or judge me. Now I can blossom and grow and learn.

(Rogers 1983)

Epilogue

> In school during an R.E. lesson about Easter, the class teacher read the account of the Last Supper and Ellie whispered, 'That was good sharing wasn't it?'

We have written the following words to express the way we would like it to be for all children:

How it seems to me...

When I am given a compliment it makes me feel happy inside.

When someone believes in me and says 'you can do it, keep going', then I stick to it and persevere and I can do it.

When someone says 'Just a minute ... rewind, try your best', then I get a chance to practise getting it right.

When I am given time and taught how to calm down then my brain has time to think and I can make the right decisions.

When I am given time to be by myself I realise that others need time on their own too.

When I use my thinking to imagine a safe place to be then I am able to shut 'Worry' out and get to sleep at night.

I like it when I know there are people around me who believe I can be successful.

I like it when other children show me that they like me and want to be my friend.

It feels good when I smile at someone and they smile back, so 'one smile makes two'.

I feel safe when I know the plan.

I like it when other people need me.

I like it when I get a 'thumbs up', or a smile or a wink because I know I am not forgotten.

When I remember 'getting it right' it helps me to manage new things.

Reflection

Our Wellie Wednesday philosophy was developed from working with many children over the years. Our experience of finding what worked for them evolved further as we met each new child and devised helpful ways of enabling them to make progress. The following words express our Wellie Wednesday philosophy and suggest ways in which it can be embedded into the classroom.

My teacher...

- Tells us how it is going to be in our classroom. We have a beliefs chart to help us remember. This helps us to feel safe and know what is expected.
- Keeps an eye on me across the room, does a thumbs up sometimes if they are busy elsewhere, sometimes they leave something of theirs on my table so I know they will come back later.
- Is fair, they explain things clearly and I know the consequences of not doing my work.
- Notices me, smiles and listens to me when it is my turn.
- Says it's OK to get things wrong. I learn from my mistakes now, I learn how not to do it!
- Notices if I pick up my pencil and start my work quickly and compliments me.
- Reminds me to use my 'thinking voice' sometimes.
- Has helped me to recognise my different parts, angry/calm/fun-loving.
- Helps me to keep 'Trouble' out, especially at playtime.
- Knows when I need a quiet space and calm activities to get me settled after a bad start to the day.
- Has a 'windows of fun' and a 'calm box' for when I need to calm down, with word searches, logic puzzles, crosswords, quizzes.
- Reminds me to 'rewind' to get things right.
- Tells me what is going to happen next and warns me if something hard or new is going to happen (we have a visual timetable to help and some things stay the same all the time).
- Knows I get hungry and thirsty before lunch and my 'grumpy part' begins to take over.
- Helps us to care for our environment. Pencils are kept sharp and we try not to drop them on the floor. We put things back where they belong.
- Keeps equipment in the same place with clear labels so I know where to find what I need for a task and can get on quickly.
- Means what she says and gives me time to take up instructions.
- Gives us two good choices: tidy it up now or sit for five minutes to think and then tidy it up.
- Wonders aloud, or commentates, and helps me to understand my feelings and name them.
- Helps me to realise it's not always my turn to speak and to give my ears a turn!
- Helps me to be kind and care about others. Says, 'What would I see you doing if you were being kind?'
- Helps me to relax using deep breaths: 7/11 breathing. I have learnt actions to go with the breathing that help my brain.
- Draws me closer when I am having a difficult time, rather than sending me further away.
- Says 'tomorrow's another day, start again!' when I've had a tricky day.
- Notices when I'm getting it right – even very small things – and gives me a compliment telling me what they have noticed, not just a well done.
- Gives me jobs to do because they know I can be trusted and I like to take some responsibility, it makes me feel part of the group and that I can make a positive

contribution. I know when it is my turn because there are notices, for example, when it is my turn to water the plants.

- Reminds me to think before I say and do things, reminds me that if I get it a bit wrong I can 'check and change'.
- Helps me to persevere when things are hard and to keep going even if I can't do it YET!
- Expects us to tell the truth. She says if you always tell the truth you do not have to remember what you said before. We know that when we tell a lie the truth is still hidden inside us.
- Is wise and thoughtful, helping us to become wise and thoughtful too.
- Is interested in my good news I can tell when I have remembered to get it right because I can see their smile and give me a compliment and record it on our class target chart.
- Says 'do your best at all times'. Sometimes they play us music to help: 'Reach for the Stars', or 'Proud?'
- I trust my teacher. They make me feel good about myself and help me to understand myself better. This helps me to enjoy school and try my best.

This book has told the story of the Wellie Wednesday project and the journeys children took with their families and schools to achieve success. By sharing their good news with others, we hope more children will be able to take positive steps forward and the good news will spread. It is hoped that the book will support practitioners, parents and carers and children, who find themselves in negative cycles and situations, to take steps forward to a positive future.

Thank you to all our Wellie Wednesday children and their families: we have not forgotten you, and we hope that you are still flying on the wings of possibility.

Reference

Proud. Heather Small. (2012)
Reach for the Stars. S Club 7. (2008)
Rogers, C. (1983). *Freedom to learn: For the 80's*. A thorough revision of Freedom to Learn, p. 125. Ohio: Merrill.

Index